Foreword by George Weigel

THE POPE

&

THE CEO

John Paul II's Leadership Lessons to a Young Swiss Guard

Andreas Widmer

Foreword by George Weigel

THE POPE
&
THE CEO

John Paul II's Leadership Lessons
to a Young Swiss Guard

Andreas Widmer

EMMAUS
ROAD
PUBLISHING

Steubenville, Ohio
A Division of Catholics United for the Faith
emmausroad.org

Emmaus Road Publishing
827 North Fourth Street
Steubenville, Ohio 43952

Library of Congress Control Number: 2011934212
ISBN: 9781931018760

Cover design
Karin Rabensteiner

Layout & Design
Theresa Westling

Cover artwork:
Servizio Fotografico-L'Osservatore Romano
Michelle Widmer–Schultz Photography

For Michelle and Elias
And in homage to Blessed Pope John Paul II

Table of Contents

Foreword

Opening the NBC News coverage of Pope John Paul II's funeral Mass on April 8, 2005, anchor Brian Williams welcomed his audience to "the human event of a generation." It was an apt phrase, not only because of the vast throngs that had flocked to Rome to say goodbye to John Paul, but because the late pope had touched human lives across a remarkable spectrum of humanity during his twenty-six and a half years as Bishop of Rome.

Andreas Widmer's was one of the lives John Paul II touched.

Andreas's own story is a compelling one of faith, success, failure, redirection, and the discovery of what is truly important in a genuinely human life. But I'll let him tell that story in the fine book you're about to read. As John Paul II's biographer, I'd like to highlight several key ideas taught by the late pope: ideas that Andreas Widmer learned (sometimes the hard way) and ideas that he now wants to share with others.

The first of these Big Ideas is that life is vocational. The word "vocation" comes from the Latin verb *vocare*, "to call," such that a vocation is a calling. It's not a career, in the conventional sense of that word. It's a matter of listening to the promptings of God, and then discerning what unique thing God has in mind for my life. John Paul II was convinced that every human life is a drama, a vocational play in multiple acts, which is playing within the larger cosmic drama of God's creative, redemptive, and sanctifying purposes. To live life as a vocational drama is to live a bracingly human life—it's the greatest of human adventures. And, as John Paul taught and Andreas Widmer learned, business can be a real vocation.

The second of these Big Ideas is that things have a purpose, even things that seem random or accidental. Nothing in our lives, John Paul used to say, is a "coincidence." What seems to be "coincidence" is really an aspect of divine providence that we don't understand yet. If we can learn to look at our lives in those terms, we'll never succumb to the most deadening of human temptations—the temptation to boredom.

The third of these Big Ideas involves expectations. From the mid-1990s on, I was constantly asked why Pope John Paul II was such a magnet for young people. One reason, I'm convinced, is that he didn't pander to the young; rather, he challenged them. In multiple variations on the same great theme, the pope would say, again and again, "Don't ever settle for anything less than the spiritual and moral greatness the grace of God makes possible in your life. You'll fail; we all do. But that's no reason to lower the bar of expectation. Get up, dust yourself off, seek forgiveness and reconciliation, and then keep trying. But don't *ever* settle for being less than the noble human being—the leader and exemplar—you can be."

Christians call that nobility "sanctity," and the challenge to nobility and sanctity that John Paul II offered was Not-For-Young-People-Only. Why? Because being a saint is every baptized person's human, as well as Christian, destiny.

When the Catholic Church beatified John Paul II on May 1, 2011, the Church was bearing public witness to its conviction that this was a life of heroic virtue, a life that could be held up for others to emulate. At the same time, the extraordinary response John Paul II drew from men and women who were neither Catholics nor Christians, nor even religious believers, bore testimony to the fact that a saintly life is a compelling human life. The saints are not men and women who have somehow leapt above the human condition; the saints are men and women who have lived fully human lives through the power of grace.

Andreas Widmer is an honest man, a good man, and an insightful man. His reflections on what he learned from perhaps the greatest Christian of our time offer all of us a powerful example of leadership at work.

—George Weigel

George Weigel is Distinguished Senior Fellow of Washington's Ethics and Public Policy Center, where he holds the William E. Simon Chair in Catholic Studies. His two-volume biography of Pope John Paul II includes *Witness to Hope* (1999) and *The End and the Beginning* (2010).

Preface

The Pope & The CEO is a guidebook for people seeking to integrate faith into all aspects of their lives. It is inspired by the example of Pope John Paul II. As a Swiss Guard in my early twenties, I was privileged to live very close to him, one of the great leaders of the 20th century. John Paul's sincerity impressed me, both in his faith and how he brought that faith to all aspects of his life. His example had a tremendous effect on my life. This book is my effort to share the lessons I learned from his example, based primarily on my memories of John Paul II during the two years I was tasked with protecting him. It also tells the story of how those memories later directed me in my quest to live my Catholic faith as a corporate executive and CEO.

There are biographical and autobiographical elements to this book. Occasional stories are not my own or are ones that I witnessed, along with the rest of the world, through the lens of the media. The book offers glimpses into the life of a Swiss Guard at the Vatican.

The pages that follow, however, are primarily intended to help the Christian executive, CEO, entrepreneur, or small business owner learn some key principles of successful leadership, as I did, at the feet of John Paul II. It is my hope that the head of any organization—family, school, church, or association—will see a ready application, and will benefit from this book and its lessons.

I myself didn't learn those lessons right away. It took me years to see the connections between the pope I once served and the work I did everyday. I had to make and lose millions of dollars before I began to understand how blessed I was by my time at the Vatican and how much John Paul II had taught me.

This book is the book I wish someone had given me twenty years ago. It makes explicit all the lessons that I had to learn the hard way, through my own failures. It also contains the lessons I'm still learning, lessons that my intellect grasps, but that are more easily understood in theory than lived in practice.

How To Use This Book

The Pope & The CEO is divided into nine chapters or lessons. Each contains several stories or reflections about John Paul II, as well as practical applications and a good dose of Church teaching. I try in each chapter to connect that teaching to the world of business and make it as relevant as possible to the experience of those tasked with leading a team of people, whether big or small.

At the end of each chapter you'll find a practical exercise, prayer, or piece of wisdom to help you live out the teaching and lessons in your life. You'll also find questions for reflection designed to help you connect the lessons of the chapter to your own experiences. If you're interested in learning more, you can visit www.thepopeandtheceo.com, where you'll find additional exercises, ideas and information on each chapter.

At that same website, you'll also find recommendations for further reading on each chapter's subject. You don't have to be a theologian or a Scripture scholar to understand the teachings outlined in this book. A great amount of background knowledge on the Catholic faith or John Paul II isn't necessary, but more knowledge is almost always a good thing; if you want to go deeper into any or all of the topics raised here, the reading lists will help you do that.

John Paul's influence made me understand that business and faith go together—they are not opposed to each other. Business can be a wonderful school of virtue and faith. What's more, faith and virtue make a business and the economy truly prosperous. The late pope is a great inspiration and example for business leaders. He is that for me and I hope he will be for you as well.

Introduction

The Pope and I:
A Swiss Guard's Story

It was almost over. I knew that. It was my decision. But it still didn't feel quite real. For two years, this had been my life, my home, my purpose, and in a few short minutes, it would all come to an end.

Four other guards were with me leaving the service that day. We waited in a small room not far from where the pope held his Wednesday audiences. We heard the noise of the crowds, the cheering and applause. Before long he would be with us, saying goodbye.

I looked around and saw my friend standing next to me. We looked like we belonged to another century—more like something out of a Renaissance painting. Two years before, when I first joined the Swiss Guards, the red, blue, and yellow striped uniform, with its puffed sleeves and full legs, had seemed strange and awkward. It was almost like I was a boy playing dress up. But now it felt familiar, comfortable. I had grown used to it over the course of my service. I'd grown used to everything that had once seemed so strange about living and working in Vatican City. And I was about to walk away from it all.

Then John Paul came in.

In the two years I'd served in the Swiss Guards, I'd seen and talked to Pope John Paul II more times than I could count. But this time was different. This was to be my last audience with him, my final chance to thank him for the opportunity to serve him. I was nervous. I was anxious about the future, anxious that I'd made the wrong decision in choosing to leave the Guards, anxious about the girl who was behind that decision.

When the pope saw me, he pretended to act surprised.

"Didn't you just start?" he said to me with a smile. "Why are you leaving already? Did I not treat you well?"

"Holy Father, I'm getting older and have to move on," was my reply.

He looked away and laughed, "Can you believe this guy? Getting old! How old are you?"

"I'm twenty-two."

"You're a kid! What are you talking about? Getting old? But if you have to leave, leave with my blessing. Go and bring Christ into the world!"

Go and bring Christ into the world. That was more than just my plan: as a former Swiss Guard, it would actually be my duty.

You see, there's a code of honor in the Guards passed from generation to generation. When you're sworn into active duty, you pledge to defend the pope with your life, to shield him with your person. But when you've gone back out into the world, it's understood that you will continue to shield him, only this time with your persona, with how you live your life.

I shook the pope's hand one last time, suddenly full of confidence. It was his confidence in me, in all of us, that I felt. I looked into his eyes, full of warmth and laughter, and I knew that would be the last time I would ever do so. At that moment, I didn't want to leave. I wanted to cry. Instead, I walked out of the room. The next day I completed my active service in the Guards, and left to do what the pope asked me to do, what I had in fact sworn an oath to do.

But did I actually do it? Did I bring Christ into the world? Did my actions, in any way, make that holy man I served proud? Or did I let him down?

Twenty years of hindsight tells me that I probably did a little bit of both.

Defenders of the Church's Freedom

When I first entered the Swiss Guards in December of 1986, I certainly wasn't thinking about bringing Christ into the world. I was thinking that being a bodyguard was about the coolest job I could imagine.

The possibility of joining the Guards had been proposed to me by one of my friends back in Switzerland. The idea intrigued me. I was nineteen at the time, and not sure what I wanted to do with my life. I'd never been all that crazy about school. Being outdoors was much more my style. But I'd done well with my training in sales and business management, and assumed that would be the direction my career would take.

I wasn't quite ready to give my life over to business yet. I wanted to do something, to go somewhere outside the small Swiss village where I'd grown up. So I got in touch with an ex-guard and went to his house for dinner. He regaled me with stories of his time in the service, and before the evening ended, I was sold. The opportunity sounded like just what I was looking for. Being Swiss, Catholic, and male, I technically answered every requirement for the job.

There is a bit more to being a Swiss Guard than that. The Swiss Guards are the pope's personal bodyguards, charged with protecting him in the Vatican and on the road. They're also responsible for keeping the Papal Palace safe, greeting visitors, and honoring the many important guests who come to the Vatican each year. Accordingly, they need to know the basics of defense strategies, weaponry, and hand-to-hand combat, and any number of details about the Vatican and its protocol.

The Swiss Guards have been performing these duties, in one form or another, since 1506, when 150 men from my homeland first reported to Rome for duty under Pope Julius II. Only a few years later, in 1527, Pope Clement VII named the Swiss Guards "Defenders of the Church's Freedom" after they saved his life during the Sack of Rome. Making a final stand, 189 Swiss Guards delayed 34,000 troops of Emperor Charles V, so that some of the Guards could bring the pope to safety. They paid a heavy price for their bravery: Only 42 of them survived to enjoy the successful completion of their plan.

Today, there are no invading armies to fend off, but there are still threats to the pope and Vatican City. There also are dignitaries to receive, tourists to manage, and honor duties to be performed. It all happens in one of the most beautiful cities in the world. How could that not appeal to a young man looking for adventure?

As soon as I finished my one-year service in the Swiss Army (something required of all Swiss men), I entered the Guards.

A World and Church In Flux

I arrived in Rome on December 1, 1986. At the time, John Paul II had been pope for just over eight years. What an eight years it had been. Internally, the Church was still fraught with dissent and conflict left over from both the Second Vatican Council and the cultural revolutions that the West experienced in the 1960s and 1970s. John Paul was under tremendous pressure to "modernize" the Church and bring its teachings in line with the secular culture.

The world was rife with tension in 1986. The Cold War was coming to a head, with America and England, in partnership with the pope, pushing mightily against the Soviet Union. Mikhail Gorbachev had recently come to power, but the Soviet war in Afghanistan still raged, and the U.S. had only just torn down its embassy in Moscow because it was so overrun by bugs…of the electronic variety, that is.

For two years, I lived and worked at the center of that spiritual and political drama. In the process I learned a great deal about the world, myself, and God.

The saying goes that Swiss Guards either lose or find their faith in Rome. I found mine. It didn't take long. Serving under John Paul II made it almost easy. He was remarkable: a scholar, an actor, an outdoorsman, a diplomat, but most of all, a strong, vibrant, loving follower of Christ. In everything he did, he bore witness to the One he served. He lived the Faith. It would have been very difficult not to be affected by that.

But, while it didn't take long for me to find my faith, it took much longer for me to figure out how to live that faith in the world. For over a decade, I struggled with how to integrate my personal faith and my professional life. I kept them separate. I paid for that, both in dollars and in currencies far more precious.

My "American Dream"

Michelle was a beautiful American girl studying in Rome and, for me, it was love at first sight. Any thoughts I'd had of the priesthood or long-term service in the Guards went right out of my head when I met her. With the help and guidance of my friend Father Peter Gori, an Augustinian priest who befriended me in Rome, I made the decision to leave the Guards and go to school in Massachusetts, where I could be near Michelle.

So, in 1989, I moved to the U.S., began studying international business, and proposed to the girl of my dreams. We married soon after, with Father Peter presiding at our wedding. At first, the deal was that Michelle would work while I went to school. But that didn't sit well with me for long. I was itching to be the provider, and at the beginning of my senior year in college, with Michelle's encouragement, I accepted an unpaid internship at a small start-up technology company. The "unpaid" part of the internship made me hesitate before accepting the offer, but Michelle urged me to go for it, saying prophetically, "When they see what you can do, they'll start to pay you."

She was right. Within a few weeks, the company welcomed me as its fifty-first employee.

The Rise

That was the summer of 1991, and the company was FTP Software. A few innovative undergraduates from MIT had started the company not long before with a great idea: Create a system that would translate Internet Protocol (IP) from large UNIX computers to desktop computers. Their work allowed PCs to access the Internet. We all know now what a huge deal that was, but at the time, I had very little grasp of what it would mean. Actually, I hardly knew how to use a computer.

But I did know there was something special about this company. The atmosphere was electric. There was a common vision. Everyone was pulling in the same direction. That's not to say that no conflicts or problems existed. They did. But we were all joined together by a common vision of making this new network called the Internet a reality. We all gave everything we had to the endeavor.

My first couple of years there, I managed to juggle work and school. I would go to work very early, deal with the European clients via phone, then head off to classes for the remainder of the day. In the late afternoon, I returned to the office to work with the Asian clients. It was crazy, but I loved it. I loved it not only because I enjoyed the work, but also because the people I worked with and for appreciated my efforts and made no secret about that. I knew I was a valuable part of a team. Sometimes I made mistakes. I was young and learning as I went. But so was just about everyone else at FTP. The strategy was to learn quickly and take advantage of every opportunity to increase our responsibilities.

The company grew rapidly. During those first few years, we doubled our revenues every year. I started traveling overseas during my school vacations to visit our resellers and customers in Europe. In 1993, I graduated from college and was named the Vice President of FTP's European subsidiary. Around the same time, FTP went public. This was one of the first large high-tech IPOs in the early nineties, and I was right there in the midst of it, having gone from unpaid intern to vice president in three short years. I was, for all intents and purposes, living the American dream. I loved it.

I continued loving it for at least another year. In 1994, FTP moved Michelle and me to Europe so that I could open the company's offices in Munich, London, and Paris, hire new staff, and start production of our software in the Netherlands. Once there, my team and I evangelized the glories of the Internet across Europe, speaking at trade shows and conferences and giving interviews to television shows and newspapers.

At the age of twenty-eight, I had over one hundred employees and managed over 100 million dollars in revenue. I flew first class, stayed at the best hotels, and lived in a luxury penthouse in Munich's most exclusive neighborhood.

I also worked seven days a week, 365 days a year, and I didn't love it any more.

The Fall

It wasn't just the hours at work that were doing me in. Sometime after going public, the culture in the company changed. We were experiencing some strong competition and were no longer growing at the same rate. That seemed logical to me since growth is measured in percentages and growing by 100, 50, or 25 percent is a lot easier to do when you're growing from a smaller number. The larger that number gets, the harder it is to sustain the same rate of growth.

I brought that up from time to time, and was not alone in seeing the sense behind it. But sense wasn't the issue. Wall Street analysts' expectations were. They were harsh taskmasters and that became the company's "end-all and be-all": Outperform the analysts' expectations for the quarter. But every time we did, it grew harder to do again. The pressure on everyone went up. Employees worked in fear of being blamed for the company's failure to meet unrealistic expectations, and innovation suffered as a result.

At first, I bought into this new way of doing business. In pursuit of reaching my ever-mounting quarterly goals, I neglected every other responsibility in my life. I lived to work. When Christmas came, I considered it a special luxury to leave Munich and spend Christmas Eve with my family in Switzerland. The next morning, however, while the family gathered to celebrate, I was itching to leave so that I could focus on my quarter-end. When my nieces and nephews headed outside to enjoy a sunny day of sledding, I hit the road for Munich, convinced I was making the most responsible and productive decision.

I was not, however, convinced for long. The culture of the company was turning poisonous. We were no longer a team working toward a common goal. We were rivals, playing against each other in a zero sum game. As the company's product began losing its competitive edge to Windows 95, I decided I'd had enough.

The Crash

I left FTP in 1996 to join Dragon Systems. The company was set to release a revolutionary product that would allow people to talk to their computers in natural speech. They hired me a year before the product's release to help them grow.

Once again I found myself working for a company with a common vision and a common passion in an environment that encouraged innovation. The company had been founded by a husband and wife team who regarded the company as a kind of family. They knew how to encourage their employees, to make them feel that they mattered and were valued. Risk taking was rewarded and long-term strategic goals pursued. We thrived, both as individuals and as a company.

On my 34th birthday, Dragon Systems was sold for over $600 million. I owned a small chunk of the stock, but enough that I wouldn't have to worry about my next job or any job after that. At least, that's what I thought.

The key decision about the monetization of my shares came during a trip to Asia. Michelle and I were in Singapore when I received a call from the Human Resources Department. I was told that the trading window during which it was legal for executives to sell company shares was about to close. They wanted to know how many shares I wanted to sell. Confident in the company's current direction, I started to say that I didn't want to sell anything. But Michelle intervened and asked me to discuss the decision with her first. I hung up and curtly told her that I knew what I was doing: The company that had acquired us had great plans, and the stock price would soar in the next six to twelve months.

Michelle had a different perspective.

"How much money do we really need?" she asked me. "Look at how the price is dropping. I don't have a good feeling about this. Let's just sell what we have and leave this crazy up and down life. We already have more than enough to live on."

But I thought I knew better. So, to calm her down, I agreed to sell a "nest egg" worth of shares and hold on to the rest. I called HR back, made arrangements for the sale, then returned my focus to the trip and the business at hand.

Two months later, a junior journalist from the Wall Street Journal found out that the company we sold Dragon Systems to was fraudulent. In another area of their business they misstated their earnings and hundreds of millions of dollars were unaccounted for. The article basically said they'd lied and cheated on a massive scale. The month after the story broke, the shares of the company were pulled off the market and the company was forced into bankruptcy, with its key managers going to jail.

I was left with Michelle, the nest egg, and a whole lot of frustration.

Back to the Beginning

The months following news of the fraud were filled with anger, confusion, and resentment. I felt like the wind had been knocked out of me. I couldn't breathe. It wasn't just the money we'd lost. It was the fact that we'd lost it because of someone else's criminal deception. They lied to our faces, and we believed them. Bitterness beckoned.

Again and again I asked myself how this could have happened. One of the most prestigious accounting firms in the world had given them a clean bill of health. And now there was no recourse? We couldn't fight back? I racked my brain trying to figure out what I could have done differently. I was there, at the very first meeting with them. Didn't I feel strange about it? I did. So why didn't I say something? Why didn't I act on my instincts?

But there was nothing I could do to change history and nothing I could do to get the wrong righted. The courts couldn't help us. Nobody could. I spent a lot of time feeling sorry for myself. I also spent a lot of time questioning the whole system of capitalism. Maybe it was wrong. Maybe I was wrong. I'd watched the drive for ever-increasing profits destroy two companies for which I'd cared deeply. Maybe the whole thing was corrupt from the start, doomed to always end this way. I felt stuck, mired in a hole of confusion and resentment, from which I couldn't escape.

One evening, in an effort to quell my gloomy thoughts, I turned on the television.

The Spirituality of Work

It was 2000, the Year of Jubilee, and the man I'd once served, John Paul II, was seen everywhere. There were so many events for the Jubilee, like World Youth Day, and so many trips to places like the Holy Land and Fatima, that the pope had become a constant media presence. I started watching his appearances, finding equal parts distraction and consolation in them. Then, one day, after a Mass for the Jubilee of Workers, John Paul II gave me the answers for which I'd been searching.

At the event, John Paul spoke of a "spirituality of work," and called people to join together in building a society that respects man and his work.

"Man is more valuable for what he is than what he has," the pope declared. He then added, "Whatever is done for the sake of greater justice, wider fraternity, and a more human ordering of social relationships counts for more than any progress in the technical field."[1]

I couldn't let go of those words. I turned them over and over in my mind. With each turn, I started to realize that it's the person, every specific human person, who counts in business. Business exists for the person, not the person for the business. Profits help a business operate, but they're not the end. Helping the human person is the end. If it weren't for the human person, we wouldn't be doing business in the first place.

There was one more quote from that Jubilee year that I couldn't forget: "In a special way the Council Fathers entrusted you with the mission 'of seeking the Kingdom of God by engaging in temporal affairs and directing them according to God's will.'"[2]

Although he was quoting from a Vatican II document, when he said that, I felt like he was speaking to me personally, calling out to me across an ocean, and repeating much the same thing he'd said during our last meeting in that ceremonial room at the Vatican twelve years before.

I decided to change my career trajectory and focus on business strategy and how that could help the poor. Maybe that industry provided more meaning than what I experienced in the business world of the West. Maybe I would find virtue there. Maybe that work would be intrinsically in line with my Christian faith.

My New Strategy
In 2001, I was hired to help the OTF Group, a burgeoning consulting firm that focused on business strategy in uncertain

environments. While its parent company, the Monitor Group, focused on large multinational companies, OTF focused on small and midsize companies that faced unpredictable and frequent change. Given my experience in the software startup space, I was a good fit for them. Yet the focus on emerging markets provided me with new challenges.

I traveled to our clients and met emerging market entrepreneurs in Africa, Latin America and the Middle East. I noticed how similar they are to any entrepreneurs I worked with here in the United States. In my four years with OTF, our projects reached from Alabama to Afghanistan, from Ontario to Rwanda, from Jamaica to Macedonia and Saó Paolo to Gabon. Wherever there was poverty, and often right after violent conflict, we advised private sector companies and governments on how to develop competitive business strategies to help them participate effectively in the global economy. I don't think I had ever felt more gratified in my work. Nor had I ever felt more convinced that my work, the work of my colleagues, and of our company was profoundly fulfilling and meaningful.

The industry as a whole, however, left me disillusioned: most development organizations I met with focused more on finding their next tranche of funding than on having a lasting impact on the people they were supposed to serve. In their work, they inadvertently bred a culture of dependency and stagnation. The prevailing paradigm of these companies and the multilaterals who funded them said it was okay to help a very poor person, but not to help that person create wealth—that would be too much. Just subsistence, no more. Having the poor become wealthy would take them away as a funding source. It wasn't said, but the actions clearly portrayed this thought. At the same time, these firms and NGOs patronize the poor. They determine what's good for people and how they should live and behave. I often thought that I don't have as much control over my own son's life as some

NGOs have over the lives of the people they supposedly help. I did not want to move further into that industry. Its shortcomings looked no different to me than the ones in the US business world I'd experienced. Just like them, they have a noble objective but on the way fall prey to selfish interests and corrupt values. I did not find the difference I was hoping for.

I felt the pull to go back into a startup venture. I loved advising others on business strategy, but the pull was to go back into business myself. I left OTF, accepting a non-paid position as an executive in residence at Highland Capital Partners, a Boston-based venture capital company. That gave me a prime space to get to know many of the current startup projects in the area, and afforded me the opportunity to get involved with a few ventures. It was a wonderful combination of circumstances, time, and place.

At the same time, I was asked by Sir John Templeton's foundation to write a business plan for them to enter into the field of enterprise-based solutions to poverty—the space that we promoted so heavily at OTF. I felt that this was a once-in-a-lifetime opportunity. One of the world's most prolific philanthropists asking me to help define a strategy to promote what I learned as a participant in emerging and innovative companies, asking me to help promote the lessons learned and best practices found during our work at OTF, and to integrate it all into a mind-set of human dignity and faith. Unbelievable!

Beginning to See the Light

I worked on two tracks—one with new ventures and the other with the Templeton Foundation on their new strategy. I knew that eventually one of them would demand a full time commitment, but I did not know which one I was meant to pursue. This time, I wanted to make my decision consciously. I wanted to do God's will, not my own. It was a two-year long process of discernment. I won't tell you here that it was an easy time. It wasn't. Discernment is difficult and uncomfortable. Though I'm looking for a "yes" to something, that "yes" entails a "no" to many other alternatives, and saying no to an opportunity is always difficult.

One and a half years after leaving OTF, the delivery of my plan to Templeton and the final Highland Capital presentations coincided. I was waiting for answers and reactions from both over the holidays of 2007.

I prayed that God would please close the doors he didn't want me to enter—to please be clear about it. He was. I tried to get my most promising start-up funded, but to no avail. After innumerable presentations and travels across the nation, it was clear that the venture community felt we did not have a compelling solution for them. We decided to change our strategy and pursue army research funding, a direction that did not require or justify my involvement. It hurt to see that door close.

Templeton's response was more positive: they felt that we had a great plan but needed to work on its implementation.

Together with my friend and OTF business partner Michael Fairbanks, we conceived the idea of the Social Equity Venture Fund (SEVEN Fund), a philanthropic foundation that promoted the idea of enterprise-based solutions to poverty. Our objectives were to invest in research of best practices, to expose what works and what doesn't work in development, and to find and promote the best entrepreneurs in emerging markets.

The basis of our approach was a series of frameworks which Mike has developed throughout his twenty-plus-year career in development. We proposed a person-centered ethic in economic development efforts. We would synthesize Mike's vast experience in emerging markets and my work in the high technology startup sector to explore and propose enterprise solutions and wealth creation efforts in emerging markets.

The wisdom of Pope John Paul II provided a key inspiration: He once voiced frustration with the current way of measuring poverty by how many dollars a day a person earns. To him, that was both demeaning and a poor way of stating the problem. He said that poverty was not so much dollars a day, but the exclusion from networks of productivity and exchange.

George Weigel, papal biographer and Catholic scholar, writes that "Wealth in the contemporary, post-industrial world is not simply to be found in resources, but rather in ideas, entrepreneurial instincts, and skills. The wealth of nations is no longer stuff in the ground; the wealth of nations resides in the human mind, in human creativity."

Hope as a means to create prosperity will prevail if the world's poor can be integrated into networks of productivity to use their "ideas, entrepreneurial instincts, and skills" productively. This is a shift from the mindset that poorer countries should spend their efforts relying mostly on extracting their nation's natural resources.

The "networks of productivity" image is in contrast to the aid model where the poor are seen as a de-humanized "problem." This model says the problem needs to be "solved" by someone other than the poor, which removes their dignity as individuals in control of their own destinies. We believe that aid money converted into investments in companies is the more effective and empowering solution with the potential to build sustainable change. "Networks of productivity and exchange" can take a plethora of forms: Internet access, Internet market places, cell phones, schools, health networks, infrastructure, etc.

Mike and I considered this definition of poverty—exclusion from networks of productivity and exchange—to be among the best. It describes both the state of poverty and the best way forward: through enabling solutions that connect the poor with networks of productivity and exchange. It became a cornerstone of our approach.

Within six months we started our new foundation and, with it, an incredible journey into the world of promoting ideas to help solve one of the world's most pressing issues.

It was then that I noticed my work and my faith coming together, becoming more explicitly related by the day. I found myself going back to John Paul's writings more frequently. What I found spoke to me with increasing clarity.

I also started remembering—recalling the days and nights I spent by his side, guarding him and watching him while I guarded.

This was a man who not only led the world's one billion Catholics, but who had taken the Church into the modern age. He held a fractured Church together when the forces of liberalism, traditionalism, secularism, feminism, and dozens of other "isms" were working hard to pull her apart. He challenged the culture's lies head-on and stared down the entire Soviet Regime. The Eastern Bloc had crumbled under the power of that uncompromisingly firm yet loving gaze. He did all that with the utmost fidelity to Christ and with the utmost love for those he served. Amazing.

I started to make sense of it all with the help of these memories—of what mattered in business, of how companies should be run, and above all, of how leaders should lead. In Pope John Paul II, I found the example of true leadership for which I'd been searching. I've tried to follow his example, leading my companies as he led Christ's faithful. I haven't been nearly as successful, but I've been a much better leader than I otherwise would have been. My companies also have enjoyed more long-term success. And most important, my wife, our son, and I have been immeasurably happier, leading richer, more joyful, and more rewarding lives.

So what did I learn from John Paul about leadership and business all those years ago?

There were nine lessons all together. The first is this: Know who you are.

Questions for Reflection

1. What have been my greatest professional successes? What did I gain? What did it cost me to achieve that success? How did it change me?

2. What have been my greatest professional failures? What did I lose? What were the sources of those failures? How did it change me?

3. How do I define success, or the "American Dream?" How, if at all, is that different from the culture's definition of success? Whose version of success am I living? What am I willing to sacrifice for that success?

Chapter One

Know Who You Are:
The Importance of Vocation

Before I formed you in the womb I knew you, before you were
born I dedicated you, a prophet to the nations I appointed you.
Jeremiah 1:5

Whatever you shall be in life, whichever calling you choose, remember,
that the fundamental calling of a human being is to have humanity.
And you must always realize that fundamental calling, always and
everywhere I fulfill my calling to the extent that I have true humanity
… Only one who is truly human is truly a child of God.
—Blessed John Paul II

W hen I entered the Swiss Guards, I was twenty years old
and, like my fellow guards, in peak physical condition.
But as fit and energetic as we were, John Paul II could
still run rings around us.

That running began before 6:00 every morning when he
would rise, pray, dress for the day, then head to his private chapel
for more time in prayer. At 7:00 a.m., small groups of visiting
dignitaries, Catholic pilgrims, or Vatican staff would join him for
Mass. After Mass, guests joined him for breakfast. An hour or two
of office work followed. Before greeting official visitors at 11:00,
he would meet briefly with linguists to review the finer points
of whatever language he would be using to speak to the visiting
crowds or dignitaries. Then the audiences began.

Epigraph. Karol Wojtyla, Address to Graduating High School Students and Working Youth (June,
1969), as quoted in Adam Boniecki, MIC, *The Making of the Pope of the Millenium: Kalendarium*
of the Life of Karol Wojtyla, (Stockbridge, MA: Marian Press, 2000), 365]

Sometimes he spoke to thousands, sometimes only a select few; yet these audiences lasted until one or two in the afternoon. Then it was on to lunch, where various Vatican staff joined him, followed by more time for prayer, with John Paul II often heading to the rooftop gardens of the Papal Palace to walk and talk with God.

After that there was more office work and more audiences, lasting right up until dinner at 8:00 p.m. when guests often dined with him. After the meal ended he would return to reading and writing and working well into the night. Sleep came around midnight or even later. Somewhere in all that, he also found time to ask a Swiss Guard about his day, chat with the sisters who cooked for him, and keep up with old friends.

That was just his Rome schedule. Compared to his schedule while traveling, it was comparatively light. John Paul II traveled far and frequently—more than any other pope in history—104 trips to 129 countries. That's 775,000 miles or the equivalent of circumnavigating the globe 32 times.

While preparing to write this chapter, I tried to remember any times I saw that schedule taking a toll on the pope. I couldn't. I recalled plenty of occasions when I was worn out with exhaustion. I remembered the guards who traveled with him returning home and just shaking their heads in wonder, saying, "I don't know how the guy does it." Not once do I recall him being bleary-eyed. In fact, it was just the opposite.

When he would return to the Vatican from weeks on the road, he didn't head straight for his rooms and collapse in exhaustion like most would. Instead, he would stop and greet all the staff who had gathered to welcome him home. Like a general reviewing his troops, he would "inspect" us, the guards lined up in honor formation, talking to us and shaking our hands as he moved down the row. He had every right and reason to walk right past us to the calm and quiet of his apartments, but he knew it was his sacred duty to make a gift of himself to us as much as to the crowds that greeted him in foreign lands.

Day in and day out, John Paul II poured himself out in response to what God asked of him. The reason he could do that, joyfully and unfailingly, was because he knew what God had made him to do. He knew his vocation.

The Three Levels of Vocations

The term "vocation" means much more than the standard dictionary definition of "a career path or line of work." It is more of a "calling" than a "job." If you had to sum up the Catholic understanding of the word "vocation" in one sentence, you could say that one's vocation is one's mission in life. It's what God made you to do.

You could also say it's what you do for God. God gave you life, and now, by means of your vocation, you give it back to him.

Either way you look at it, your vocation gives meaning to your life. According to John Paul II, your vocation answers the question, "Why am I alive?" Moreover, he believed, only when you're living out your vocation can you find fulfillment in this life. Your vocation, understood, embraced, and lived, is what makes you feel truly and fully alive.[3]

The Universal Vocation

That's the simple explanation of vocation, but there's still a lot more to the concept. There are three different levels of vocations. They focus on different aspects of your life, and differ in importance.

The first of these three is the universal vocation. This is the vocation in which we all share. It doesn't matter who you are or where or when you live, you have the same universal vocation as every other human being on the planet: To know, love, and serve God in this life so that you can know, love, and serve him eternally in the next life. Your objective is to receive grace now so that you can receive glory later, or even more simply put, to cooperate with God in his work to save your soul.

God calls all of us to be co-creators with him as part of that cooperation. He charges us with giving life to others: either physical life or spiritual life. He charges us with giving life to ideas: creating works of art, gadgets and products, or systems of thought and service. That co-creation, John Paul II believed, is the essence of love, the fullest realization of the possibilities inherent in man. He described our ability to give life—to give birth, to invent, create, conceive, and build—as the true "grandeur" of love. When we create, we are doing that for which God made us. We're carrying out our mission and making a gift of our life to God.[4]

Primary Vocation

After the universal vocation, it starts to get more specific. After all, it's one thing to say all Christians share in the vocation to love, but it's another thing to actually live that vocation. How we live it, the way of life in which we love and serve God and others, is our primary vocation. According to the Catholic Church, there are four primary vocations: married life, dedicated single life (living in the world), the priesthood, and consecrated life (living in community).

Each of these vocations is a permanent and freely chosen way of life. Each also entails a gift of self. In choosing a primary vocation, you make your inalienable and non-transferable "I" someone else's property. In other words, you give priority in your life either to God and the consecrated life or to your spouse and family.

This gift of self gives your life a concrete direction and purpose. It orders your desires, priorities, and responsibilities, at least in a general way. If I'm married and have a child, I'm responsible not only for myself, but also for my spouse and child. I'm called to provide for their physical and material needs. I'm also called to provide for their intellectual, emotional, and spiritual needs. The care of their souls, as well as their bodies, is entrusted to me. It's my "job" to help them get to heaven, just as it's their "job" to help me get to heaven. The choices I make, the actions I take, and the responsibilities I undertake are all decisions that have to be made in light of my responsibilities to them.

The same goes for priests and those living a religious life. A religious sister considers the good of her community before her own good. Her path to heaven is paved by the rules and obligations of her life with the other sisters. A priest is likewise tasked with providing for the spiritual well-being of his parishioners and supporting his bishop in teaching and defending the Faith. How he orders his life and time needs to be directed to those larger ends.

Our modern notions of freedom can confuse us about the value of this kind of vocation. So often, we see the type of limitations to our freedom that a permanent commitment brings as impediments to "being who we are." But real freedom isn't freedom from outside restrictions. Real freedom is the freedom to love and give ourselves fully. Freedom in fact exists for the sake of love. It is the means to the end we all desire—loving communion with God and others. It is when we give ourselves most fully that we fulfill ourselves most effectively. That's when we're truly free.[5]

Secondary Vocation

Your universal vocation gives you the overarching purpose of your life, your ultimate goal. Your primary vocation gives you a framework for achieving that goal. It sets certain parameters or, to phrase it a bit differently, lays out a path for you to follow on your journey to heaven. The third level of vocation, your secondary vocation, is what you do on that path. It's how you use your gifts and talents in service of God and others while living out your universal and primary vocations. For most of us, this means our work or profession. It also, however, can apply to your civic and community involvement, apostolate work, or simply bearing the various crosses and trials that come your way in life. It's your plan of action for living.

When it comes to work, John Paul II believed that our profession is integral to who we are as human beings. He said that not just of seemingly exciting and important professions, such as being the pope, but also of the harshest forms of manual labor. When it comes to labor, John Paul knew of what he spoke. Growing up in Poland during World War II, the one-day pope worked long hours in a lime quarry and a chemical plant. He knew from those experiences just how challenging work could be.

But he also knew what happened when work was taken away from man or when man was not free to pursue the work for which God made him. He learned that as a seminarian, priest, and bishop in Soviet-dominated Poland, where economic centralization led to the elimination of private property and ended entrepreneurial activity.

John Paul saw freedom curtailed, workers denigrated, and human dignity violated. He came to realize that in order to become the person God made us to be, we each had to be free to choose, free to create, and even free to fail in our professional lives. John Paul argued that when we do that, when we freely pursue the work for which we were made, and which our gifts, talents, nature, and circumstances suit, we discover who we really are.[6]

John Paul II likewise realized that through our work we don't simply make more: We become more. Work shapes us, refines us, and pushes us to discover and hone our natural gifts. It enables us to love, becoming a means by which we're able to serve our family, customers, clients, neighbors, and communities. Through that, work becomes a means of giving our life to God.

When you think of work in that way, you can see that, like your primary vocation, it too is not a constraint upon your freedom. It's not something that keeps you from doing what you really love— fishing, cooking, or checking the box scores for the Boston Red Sox. It's something that enables you to live more fully the life God intended you to live.

The fact that work is sometimes difficult, monotonous, or downright painful doesn't lessen its efficacy in that endeavor. It enhances it. All the difficulty, monotony, and pain you face are things you can unite to the work, Passion, and death of Christ. They are something you can, to quote centuries of Catholic mothers, "offer up" in order to obtain grace for yourself and others.

That ability is a holy thing. Work can, in fact, be a holy thing. All work, not only that of priests and religious, can be holy when done as an act of love, service, and sacrifice according to the mind of God. That's what the Incarnation made possible. That's why St. Thomas Aquinas could say with such confidence, "There can be no joy in living without joy in work."

The Chaos of Competing Priorities

So why does all this vocation stuff matter? What does understanding it have to do with leading a company or small business?

The answer is, "Everything."

What John Paul II understood so well—his universal (his call to holiness), primary (his priesthood), and secondary vocation (his being a priest, bishop, and then pope)—is the very thing most of us spend our entire lives trying to figure out. We want to know who we are, why we exist, and what we were made for. Those are eternal questions asked by every man in every age. Answering them is never easy, and all the demands of life—the competing roles we play and priorities we juggle—make answering them harder still.

Everyone—whether you're a pope leading millions, a CEO leading hundreds, or a father leading a few—wears more than one hat in this life. You are an employer or employee, but you're also a son or daughter, brother or sister, husband or wife, mother or father, community leader or volunteer, citizen or soldier, neighbor or friend. The list goes on and on. All these various roles give you multiple ways to serve others and use your gifts. They also, however, create multiple sets of expectations and goals. Those expectations and goals often conflict.

To start with, they pull you in opposite directions, each demanding time from the other. They also seem to require opposite virtues. What it takes to get ahead in business can seem a far cry

25

from what it takes to be a good father or Christian disciple. Each role comes with a culture of competing priorities. For example, what the culture of corporate success tells you is important—long hours at the office, cut-throat business instincts, and quarterly benchmarks—is different from what the culture of parenthood says matters most—saving money, being present at home, and modeling responsibility, commitment, and love for your children.

Most of us at least try to balance our different roles and the priorities that accompany them, working hard to do what's expected of us at work, home, and in our communities, making every effort to please our boss, our spouse, and our kids. But in trying to please everybody, we can end up feeling like we're pleasing nobody.

In order to be successful in competing cultures, we can also start acting like one person at the office and another person at home. We compartmentalize, live a "duality" that allows one set of values and beliefs to guide us in our professional lives and another in our personal lives.

We often make trade-offs, compromises, negotiated attempts, to navigate through multiple worlds. Those trade-offs can cost us dearly. I can't count the number of executives I've known over the years whose success in business has cost them the affection and respect of their wives and children, and too often their entire relationships. I've known others who've neglected their real professional passions in pursuit of a higher salary or more prestigious title. Even those who manage to strike a seemingly reasonable balance are often worn out from their efforts. They're not happy. They're exhausted. The passion they once felt for their work, hobbies, or volunteer activities first diminishes, then disappears.

Disappointment, confusion, fragmentation, and ultimately, exhaustion—that's what you set yourself up for when you don't have a clear hierarchy of roles and priorities.

The Way Out of the Chaos

When you understand all three levels of vocation, however, and the place each one holds in the hierarchy of importance, it becomes much easier to order your life and your priorities, pursuing the virtues you most need, and balancing competing roles without compromise.

John Paul II was living proof of that.

While serving in the Swiss Guards, one of my friends who had been there much longer than I had told me a story about John Paul II's first days as pope. On his first official day "on the job," with the weight of the world suddenly placed on his shoulders, John Paul made a decision. A friend and fellow Polish bishop was sick and he wanted to see him. But that's not quite right. He didn't just want to see him. He believed he was *supposed* to see him. He thought, on that day, at that moment that seeing his friend was the most important thing for him to do. So, despite the loud objections of his staff, he did just that. The world kept on turning. The most important needs were met, and the less important waited.

A few days later, at a press conference for two thousand journalists, John Paul again went his own way. After offering the expected few comments, rather then leaving, he plunged into the crowd and began chatting with the press corps. Some poor monsignor, tasked with keeping the pope on schedule, tried to pull John Paul II away. But the pope waved him off and announced into a reporter's camera, "There are people here telling me it's time to leave now. I'm the pope. I'll leave when I want to leave."

That's the difference a clear understanding of all three levels of vocation and their relationship to one another can make. John Paul considered first and foremost what God was asking of him, and then he did it. He put God first, his vocation to the priesthood second, and the many demands of the papal office third. He prayed, said the Mass, then did everything else. He did "everything else" with the same spirit that he prayed and offered Mass. That is to say, he let the duties and values of his universal and primary vocation shape how he fulfilled his secondary vocation. His energies never lagged, his passion never waned.

Finding Your Balance

Most of us will never become pope, but each of us will be able to put these priorities of vocations into action, just as the pope did. In his understanding of vocation, John Paul II found the balance between competing roles and priorities. He knew what mattered and why. He lived every day according to that knowledge. There was no confusion, no fragmentation. Everything was ordered rightly. Nothing was compartmentalized. He was the same man in front of millions that he was in front of a single lowly bodyguard.

You need to strive for the same balance as a layperson and business leader. Knowing your universal, primary, and secondary vocation will do for you what John Paul II's knowledge of his vocation did for him. It will order your commitments correctly. It will help you live according to the right values and strive for the right virtues. It will help you live an integrated life and work for the things that really matter. Above all, it will help you give yourself passionately and without reserve to what God is calling you to do and be.

That doesn't mean that you won't ever occasionally work late at the office when you'd rather be home, or that you won't miss saying your usual night prayers from time to time because you're up with a sick child. There are times when one vocation demands a higher priority, even if, technically speaking, its usual place is somewhat lower on the vocational totem pole. But knowing your vocation does prevent those occasions from becoming a way of life. It also ensures that the right value system, the value system that goes along with your universal vocation, is always shaping the way you live your primary and secondary vocations. In effect, it is your fail-safe when the temptation to compromise your values arises. It's what you can always rely on to know the right course of action and find inspiration for why you're doing what you're doing. It's an unfailing guide when questions or doubts inevitably come.

***

That's the lesson I should have learned on February 11, 1987. On that day I was looking forward to some time off, when my commanding officer broke the bad news. Due to a change in schedules, I needed to replace another guard and serve at a papal Mass. I was furious, and when I took my place beside the open-air altar in St. Peter's Square, I was seething with resentment.

For the next hour and a half, while John Paul II prayed the Mass, I stood beside him, still as a statue, but utterly absorbed in my own anger. When he issued the final blessing, I heaved a sigh of relief. Finally, the Mass was over and I could get on with my day off. But as the pope was preparing to head back into the Vatican, he looked out into the crowds. Then, he reversed course.

Descending the stairs into St. Peter's Square, John Paul began walking among the pilgrims. He would stop, greet someone, bless him, then move on to the next person. With each blessing, my anger grew. I felt almost as if he was taking his sweet time simply to make me crazy. My feet hurt, my back ached, and sweat poured down my face. My impatience boiled over.

Then, for half a second, I glanced over at the person he was blessing. To say the man was disabled would be an understatement. He had no arms, no legs, and was terribly malformed. An interpreter communicated with him by touching him in certain ways and sequences. I then realized this person was also blind and deaf. Despite all that, the look on his face at that moment was one of pure joy. The guy radiated it.

I then looked at the pilgrims next to him. There were wheelchairs and hospital beds as far as the eye could see, filled with sick souls wanting more than anything to see the pope. Suddenly I was happy to have legs that hurt.

More time passed. The pope continued down the aisle, blessing every pilgrim he could. I no longer minded. I'd been so caught up in what I wanted, what I thought was important, that I'd been blind to the very real needs right before my eyes. Not John Paul II, who didn't get days off and probably had far less sleep than I had the night before. He knew what was important. He knew what his vocation called him to do and he did it without question.

Thanks be to God for that.

Finding Your Three Vocations

- God made each of us to do something unique, something that nobody else before or after us was made to do and that nobody else can do quite as well. He made us that way both for our own personal benefit and to build up the Body of Christ in the world. How do we know what he made us to do?

- No matter what our calling, our vocation is the way in which we give back to God what he has given to us. It's a bit like when you give your child art materials—paper, brushes, pencils, colors, glitter, glue, scissors, wiggle eye stickers and pom-poms—and then ask him or her to "use all this material and make something great. Go ahead—be creative!" You then wait excitedly until your daughter or son comes back and proudly presents the latest creation. You of course love it and, just as proudly, display it at your office or in your kitchen.

- What God gives you are not art supplies, but the talents, likes, dislikes, the exact place in space and time that you live, the many specific opportunities and challenges that you encounter… and he's telling you: "Take all of this and make something good and beautiful—I got all these ingredients especially for you—do something great. I can't wait to see what you come up with!" We of course go about this in a bit more organized fashion that a child does with paint, but we should not forget to use the same awe-filled and confident approach.

30

The process of discernment is an art, not a science, and it takes time and practice to become adept at it, but these two steps are a good place to start.

Step 1: Read God's Instruction Manual: The Bible

In the Bible, we see salvation history unfold. We learn about God the Father's plan of salvation, Jesus' mission of redemption, and the Holy Spirit's work of sanctification. In the Bible, God speaks. If you need help finding your vocation, the help is there. If you need help understanding your vocation, the help is there. If you need help succeeding at the vocation to which you're already committed, the help is there.

Step 2: Follow St. Ignatius of Loyola's Advice

Ignatius, the founder of the Jesuit order, was a superb spiritual guide. His book "The Spiritual Exercises" is a must-have for any spiritual seeker. In it, he describes three steps to discernment.

First, cultivate awareness. That means you have to work on being open to God's presence in your life, believing he's there and wanting to communicate with you. One way to do this is at the end of the day ask yourself how you feel spiritually about what's going on in your life. How are you reacting, at your core, to the circumstances of life?

Second, cultivate understanding. This comes through reflecting on your reactions. Ask God what feelings are from him and what feelings are not from him. In doing that, you'll start to realize what makes you truly happy and truly sad. You'll start to hear God's voice directing you through both your emotions and your reason.

Third, take action. Use your will to choose what God wants for you and reject what he doesn't want.

Questions for Reflection

1. What's the next step on your path to holiness? Make a plan of how you can grow in holiness tomorrow. Make a plan with goals for the week, the month, and the year.

2. What is your primary vocation? What are five specific small or bold ways you can live out this vocation each day?

3. What is your secondary vocation? Make a list of the talents, opportunities, and ideas God has given you in support of that vocation. Do you see your job as an expression of that vocation? Do you feel like that child doing artwork or do you feel that your work is burning you out? Why or why not? If so, what needs to change for you? A new career? Different responsibilities? A different attitude on your part?

Chapter Two

Know God:
The Power of Prayer

Rejoice always. Pray without ceasing. In all circumstances give
thanks, for this is the will of God for you in Christ Jesus.

1 Thessalonians 5:17–18

*Prayer helps us to rediscover the loving face of God. He never abandons
his people but guarantees that, notwithstanding trials and suffering,
good triumphs in the end.*

—Blessed John Paul II

O n a winter's night in 1987, I stood in full dress uniform
inside one of the Vatican's smaller chapels. Gathered
there were between fifty and one hundred people. They
had come to join John Paul II for a prayer service that would be
broadcast around the world via Vatican Radio.

I was there in my official capacity, to guard the pope, not
pray, so while he and the visitors kept their eyes closed and heads
bowed in prayer, my eyes remained wide open. John Paul knelt
almost directly across from where I stood, and it was on him that
I focused. My focus, however, wasn't purely professional. There
was something more behind the intensity with which I watched
him. I suppose it was curiosity. I was still new at the Vatican and
still trying to figure this pope out, trying to understand who he
was and what made him tick.

That night, I got my answer.

Epigraph. Wednesday General Audience (January 26, 2005).

As I watched him pray, softly speaking the words of the Rosary, he began radiating a sense of peacefulness and calm unlike anything I had ever encountered. The longer he prayed, the more absorbed in the prayer he became, until he seemed completely taken up in it, as if nothing and no one in the room could pull him back from the place where he'd gone. He was obviously still physically present, but his spirit seemed to be someplace else.

I'd never seen anyone pray like that before. I didn't know it was possible. Up until that evening, I had always thought of prayer as an act of the imagination, a mental fantasy people cooked up to feel better about something, almost like a child talking to an imaginary friend. But there was nothing imaginary about what I saw that night. This man wasn't faking his immersion in God. What I saw was profoundly real and exceedingly desirable.

Over the course of the next two years, I watched John Paul II pray on countless occasions. I learned a great deal about prayer from watching him—what prayer is, how to pray, and what prayer accomplishes. I also learned a great deal about the pope himself through watching him pray. I discovered that prayer was at the heart of everything he did. It shaped him, guided him, and gave him the strength to lead. Prayer is what made John Paul II the man, the pope, and the leader he was. It enabled him to inspire so many so profoundly. Prayer can do the same for you and me.

The Nature of Prayer

I once overheard John Paul II say that prayer is a learned ability, something anyone can do if he only try. In other words, prayer is not an activity solely reserved for mystics and saints or priests and nuns. It's also not something to do just on Sundays or before meals. It's something for everyone, at any time.

The reason for that lies in the nature of prayer. You see, prayer isn't so much about the words you say as it is about whom you say them to. At its heart, prayer is an encounter with a Person. It's an exchange between you and God. All that goes into an exchange between any two people goes into an exchange between you and the Lord of the universe: listening, talking, or just silently being together.

When John Paul II prayed, that's what happened. He talked with God about both his own and the world's struggles, sorrows, and joys. He listened for what God had to say. He also praised God, telling him how much he loved him and thanking him for all his good works, great and small. Above all, he just basked in the joy of God's presence, much like two friends do.

That's prayer: an encounter with God to which every human being is called.

There are different ways of praying—different forms of prayer. There's vocal prayer, which is reciting specific prayers, like the Our Father or the Hail Mary. There's also mental prayer, which is more like a conversation with God. Then there's meditation, where you prayerfully reflect on a passage from Scripture or a truth of the Faith. Finally there's contemplation, where God brings you into a state of absorption in him, kind of like when two lovers become lost in each other's eyes.

According to Catholic teaching, all those various forms of prayer have value. You never grow out of or get past needing to pray vocal prayers such as the Rosary. You never become too holy or wise to present your needs to God in mental prayer. Think of it this way: A wife never tires of hearing her husband say, "I love you," no matter how many years they've been married. A father never wants his son to stop communicating his needs and struggles to him, no matter how old the son gets. The same goes for God. He neither wants nor expects you to stop saying the prayers you learned as a child or being honest with him about what you desire and fear.

The reason for that, however, isn't that God needs to hear fifty Hail Marys or he wouldn't know what you wanted if you didn't tell him. In the end, prayer isn't for God's benefit at all. It's for your benefit.

The Necessity of Prayer

God wants you to pray because you need prayer. You need to be in relationship with him. It's what you were made for. Prayer brings you into that relationship. It nourishes it, sustains it, and helps it grow.

Prayer also changes you, or more accurately, it helps you become the person God made you to be. When you pray you learn from God. You hear his voice leading you, and that helps you make wise choices. It becomes your compass, always guiding you to the "true North." That same voice roots you in the real meaning and purpose of your life. It reminds you who made you and for what purpose he made you. "Our life can only be comprehended, has meaning only when it is considered in its relationship to God. Without it, our life splinters into a thousand problems of relative importance,"[7] John Paul explained.

That's why all the various forms of prayer matter. You need vocal prayers in the same way a husband and wife need regular expressions of their love for one another. Lest we forget: marriage is a reflection of the Trinity, so what we do in a great marriage is a good analogy to how we are invited to interact with God. Saying a Rosary every morning is, in some ways, like the husband who brings his wife coffee every morning. It's a daily habit of love. Love needs those daily habits. It needs routines. We all need routines. They order our lives and help keep us on the right path. Vocal prayers do just that. They form us in the habit of faith.

Likewise, we need mental prayer. We need to talk to God, to communicate with him about what's taking place in our minds and hearts, because we need to hear his voice speaking to the problems of our day. That's why it's important that mental prayer never become a mere rattling off of our wish lists to God. It needs to be a real conversation, with intense periods of listening.

We need meditation, with the insights intense reflection brings and the connections it can help us make between the events of Scripture or the teachings of the Church and the realities of our own life. We likewise need contemplation: We need to rest in God's presence and learn to receive the grace that he wants to give us.

Prayer and the Pope

In all those ways, prayer shaped the leadership that John Paul II exercised in the Church.

First, prayer reordered his vision, helping him see all the events of his life and papacy in light of God's plan. This, for example, is why he was able to thank God for the attempt on his life made by Ali Agca in 1981.

On May 13 of that year, while greeting pilgrims in St. Peter's Square, John Paul was shot at close range by the Turkish assassin.[8] He credited his narrow escape from death to the intercession of the Virgin Mary. The actual day of the assassination attempt was one of her great feast days, the memorial of Our Lady of Fatima. On that day, sixty-four years before, Mary predicted the fall of godless Communism in Russia. John Paul saw no coincidence in that. Instead, he saw the assassination attempt and his recovery as a sign. That sign, understood through prayer, clarified his vision and made him more resolute in his stand against communism.

John Paul II saw all the great struggles of his life that way—the loss of his mother at a young age, the early death of his brother and then father, his persecution at the hands of the Nazis and the Soviets. All were experiences that could easily have destroyed another man's faith or made him bitter and hard. Prayer enabled John Paul II to see those events in light of God's love, as preparation for the service he was eventually called to give God and his Church.

Prayer is also what guided John Paul II. During the years I served him and long after, he would do his brainstorming and much of his writing in his private chapel, in front of the Eucharist. He also spent hours laying prostrate in prayer. He would praise God, be with God, petition God, and present to God the events and problems he faced. In prayer, he would reflect on what others had said to him, what others wanted him to do. When he left the chapel, he would act based upon the knowledge and understanding he gained during those hours.

When you ask people who met John Paul II in person what their impressions were of their meeting, almost invariably they'll say how intensely he focused on them. "As if I were the only person in the world," is the phrase most often heard. That too came from prayer. Prayer made John Paul II a better listener. In learning to be still and focus on God, he also learned how to be still and focus on others, to set everything else aside and be in the moment.

In the later years, when I would visit the Vatican or call a friend there and ask how the pope was doing, I would hear that his physical state was increasingly frail, that he was slowly becoming a prisoner in his own body. The strong, athletic man I'd served was slipping away. As the physical world lost its hold on him, eternity tightened its grip.

"He comes out of prayer to do what we need him to do, then goes back into prayer," a friend once told me.

Prayer, up until the very end, was John Paul II's home base. He didn't retreat into prayer to escape from the demands of his aides and the world, but rather to be alone with God, whom he loved above all else.

Those hours alone with God fed that love. They taught him who God was. They revealed his glory, his merciful heart, and his fatherly compassion. All that was revealed to John Paul II in prayer was shared with the world. Because he knew who God was, he could present the Catholic faith in a positive, optimistic way—not as a set of rules or limitations, but as the merciful path to Christ himself.

That's how he presented the Faith to the world, and that's how he presented it to me. In our conversations, he wasn't a stern or authoritarian figure, lecturing me and making me feel inadequate. He was like a coach, urging on one of his athletes. His own confidence in God's love and mercy came through in our talks and made holiness seem not necessarily easy, but at least possible. That's also why he canonized and beatified so many men and women: 1,345 priests, religious, and lay people were declared "Blessed" during his papacy, and 483 were declared saints. He wanted to show the world that God didn't call just the first Christians to holiness. He calls all of us to holiness and gives all his children the grace to become so.

People heard what John Paul II was saying. They came to believe because of his witness. They came to understand because of his teaching. Countless lives have been changed because of the man and leader John Paul II was. He was the man and leader he was primarily because of his relationship with God, a relationship forged and sustained through prayer.

Prayer and the CEO

It takes more to run a business or manage a team than just prayer. All the prayer in the world is not going to make up for a lack of skill. Piety does not replace expertise or knowledge. It enhances it.

It does that in two primary ways.

First, prayer can be a source of guidance. The more you pray, the more you learn to discern God's voice. When multiple options are before you, whether it's making a new hire, choosing a new business partner, or launching a new product, you usually consult someone—advisors, partners, or a spouse. You want someone's input other than your own. Well, God also has input to give. Almost always, he has some wisdom or insight to impart that will help you in your decision. Taking that decision to prayer is how you get the input he offers.

That input is as much about you as it is about the decision itself. You gain self-knowledge in prayer. You can learn why you're leaning toward hiring a specific person or why you're leery about making a certain deal. Once, in prayer, I realized that I was letting a past experience unfairly influence how I was interacting with someone. Another time, I came to understand that the reason I didn't want to make a deal wasn't because the deal was bad, but because I didn't like the direction and values of the other company involved. Those are the sorts of guidance prayer can give.

Seeking God's perspective also helps you better understand the people you work with and for. You learn to see them with his eyes. You're forced to contemplate how he would have you solve a problem or resolve difficulties and check your own, often imperfect, impulses to react out of anger or frustration. You're also forced to consider what's just and what's merciful. Prayer is a tool for justice and mercy, helping you to treat others with both—in the right degrees and right ways at the right time—because it connects you with God, who is justice and mercy.

Prayer isn't, however, a magic wishing well or a vending machine for spiritual wisdom. Sometimes God doesn't respond right away. When you ask for help or understanding, there might be only silence. That too is a form of guidance. It slows you down, delays action until the time is right, and teaches you the importance of patience.

In all those ways, prayer serves as a powerful guide to running a successful business and living a happy life. Even more important than receiving guidance from God is what asking for that guidance does to you.

A School for Humility

When we pray we acknowledge our dependence on Another. We acknowledge that God is the Creator, and we are merely creatures, living in service to Someone far greater than ourselves. What prayer teaches us is the virtue of humility. There are few virtues more important for any leader.

Without humility, it's easy for whatever you're doing to become all about you. Success becomes all about you. Failure becomes all about you. Decisions become all about you. The more this mindset takes hold of a leader, the more he forgets the real purpose of his work. He forgets the customers he serves and the people he leads. He forgets he's not just leading a team, but that he's a part of a team and ultimately responsible for that team's livelihood. That forgetfulness manifests itself in things like separate elevators and entrances for the CEO and any number of other perks designed to insulate leaders from the rest of the business. It also manifests itself in reckless, prideful, and unreflective decision-making.

Making business decisions just for the short-term and not the long-term causes untold damage to a company. Even more damaging are the decisions based on the owner's or CEO's pride. Pride destroys perspective. It leads you not only to think that you know best, but also that you, in fact, are the only one who knows anything at all.

Years ago, when I was still with FTP Software, the head of our company decided to purchase another company based in my territory. The company purchased was a mess—poorly run, poorly staffed, and permeated by a culture of deception. I knew this. Everyone familiar with the company knew this. But the CEO never asked me. He assumed he knew best and our company later paid the price for his pride.

Another company I once worked for had an unbelievable opportunity to partner with a young, cutting-edge firm. The CEO passed up that opportunity. He said he didn't want to "deal with those kids." What he didn't want was to admit that some start-up staffed by a bunch of newcomers could help us. Again, pride.

Long ago, in the Garden of Eden, the serpent played upon the pride of Adam and Eve, bringing about their fall from grace. He told them not to worry about what God said, to do what they wanted, that everything would be okay. The same thing goes on in businesses big and small today. Pride runs amok. It feeds delusions. It makes people think they're invincible and above the petty rules and obligations by which others must abide. It also makes them forgetful of their responsibilities and blinds them to the wisdom and talents others have to offer.

The only antidote to pride is humility, and honest prayer always produces that virtue. It reminds us of our dependency on God, grace, and the gifts he gives us through others. It also produces leaders who know themselves, know God, and know others with a clarity and wisdom that can't be attained merely through human effort. Prayer nourishes leaders with the grace they need to lead.

***

John Paul II once wrote that many people told him that they didn't know how to pray. His response was always the same. "Everyone can pray," he would say. "It is simple. The important thing is that you keep doing it."[9]

Most of us have little say about the quality of our prayers. The quality is a gift of grace that comes from God. What we do have a say in, however, is how much we pray. We can choose to make a habit of relying on God. We can choose to go to him again and again, to build a relationship. Or we can choose to ignore him.

Every time you pray you choose God. The more you make that choice, the easier prayer becomes. The easier prayer becomes, the more you'll find yourself praying. It's a circle, but it's a circle of grace, with God leading you more and more, often in ways unknown or unseen.

I discovered this truth when I was still a Swiss Guard, and John Paul II gave me a beautiful rosary, one with his special Salvador Dali Crucifix on the end. "Pray this prayer. It is my favorite prayer," he said to me then.

I took it, but without having the slightest clue what to do with it. Another priest at the Vatican eventually taught me how to pray the Rosary, and I slowly started practicing what he taught me. I came to love that prayer too, and through that prayer, came to understand so much about God and his will for my life, including that he was calling me to leave the Guards and marry Michelle.

Today, I still carry that rosary in my pocket wherever I go. It's a reminder to pray and an aid to prayer. It's more than that. Over the years I've developed the habit of holding it in my hand when I'm in conversation with people at work. It reminds me to listen to people while they talk, to wait for them to say what's really on their mind, and to think before speaking. Most of all, it reminds me of God and my dependence on him. Remembering that is a prayer in itself.

Practical Prayer

Looking to deepen your prayer life? These tips can help.

1. *Be aware.* Before you pray, focus on the fact that God is present and listening. Throughout your time in prayer, continue to cultivate an awareness of his presence.

2. *Slow down.* When reading the Scriptures or the writings of Church fathers, Doctors, and saints, don't race from passage to passage. Treat the reading like a love letter from God, savor the text, and ask God to help you understand the connection between the words on the page and the circumstances in your life and heart.

3. *Praise always.* Don't take God's goodness or love for granted. Thank him by acknowledging all that he is and all he's done for you.

4. *Tell him you're sorry.* You don't have to wait for confession to examine your conscience. Make a habit of doing this nightly. Then express contrition to God and ask for the grace to do better the next day.

5. *Be attentive.* Listen for God's voice in the movements of your soul, cultivating an awareness of feelings of consolation and desolation (joy and sorrow) as you pray.

6. *Plan for prayer.* Don't let a day go by without making time for God. Schedule a daily appointment with God and never miss it. Also, cultivate a rhythm of prayer throughout the day: praying the *Angelus* at noon, grace before meals, and small invocations such as "Lord, come to my assistance" before beginning difficult tasks.

7. *Pray in all things.* Make your life a prayer by making a gift of yourself. This can include regular fasting and acts of renunciation, giving generously to those in need, and setting aside your own plans to assist another. Every time you make one of these sacrifices, great or little, say silently, "Lord, I give this to you."

Questions for Reflection

1. Describe your ideal prayer life. When do you pray? How? Where? How often? Make a six-month outline and put your plan into reality.

2. Have you ever turned to God for help in a difficult situation, either at work or at home? Describe the difference that made.

3. Describe a difficult situation at work where you did not ask God for help or guidance? Why? What happened as a result?

4. What are at least three ways that praying more about your work and decision-making could make you a better leader?

Chapter Three

Know What's Right:
Ethics and the Human Person

So for one who knows the right thing to do and does not do it,
it is a sin.

James 4:17

*Each person, in some way, is called to work for the common good,
constantly looking out for the good of others as if it were his own.*
—Blessed John Paul II

On June 6, 1987, I was assigned to honor guard duty at
the entrance of the Papal Palace. Typically this is not the
most exciting of a Swiss Guard's tasks. The purpose of
the task is noble enough: You're considered a representative of the
Holy Father at the entrance to his home and your mere presence is
a sign of respect to special guests and dignitaries. The task doesn't
require you to do anything or say anything. You just stand there.

On this particular day, however, honor guard duty promised
a bit more excitement.

A convoy of thirty-two cars slowly pulled in as I stood next
to the stairs in the San Damaso courtyard. Out of one of the
cars stepped President Ronald Reagan and his wife Nancy. They
were greeted by Bishop Dino Monduzzi, Prefect of the Papal
Household, and introduced to a line of Vatican dignitaries, which
included the commander of the Swiss Guards. Then, after Reagan

---

Epigraph. Message for the Celebration of the World Day of Peace (January 1, 2005).

gave a crisp, military wave to the line of Guards assembled in his honor, the first couple proceeded toward the steps where I stood.

Since I was tasked with doing my best impression of a living statue, I couldn't even turn my head to get a good look at the fortieth president of the United States, then the most powerful man in the world and an icon of freedom and democracy during the height of the Cold War. Out of the corner of my eye, however, I watched him and his wife pass. They were happy, smiling, confident, and, surprisingly, much older than they appeared on television.

A few hours later, the pair reemerged from the Papal Palace, having met first with Cardinal Casaroli, the Vatican Secretary of State, and later with the pope himself. Nobody knows exactly what went on in their meeting that day, what issues the pope and the president discussed behind closed doors. But just two days later, standing in front of the infamous Brandenburg Gates, Ronald Reagan delivered what was perhaps the most remembered speech of his presidency.

"Mr. Gorbachev," he declared, "tear down this wall."

The Power of Moral Vision
Those are the words everyone knows from Reagan's speech. Lesser known are the words he spoke at the end.

> The totalitarian world produces backwardness because it does such violence to the spirit, thwarting the human impulse to create, to enjoy, to worship. The totalitarian world finds even symbols of love and of worship an affront. Years ago, before the East Germans began rebuilding their churches, they erected a secular structure: the television tower at Alexander Platz. Virtually ever since, the authorities have been working to correct what they view as the tower's one major flaw, treating the glass sphere at the top with paints and chemicals of every kind. Yet even today when the sun strikes that sphere—that sphere that

towers over all Berlin—the light makes the sign of the cross. There in Berlin, like the city itself, symbols of love, symbols of worship, cannot be suppressed.

Those words were probably written long before Reagan's meeting with John Paul II. And yet, I know they still have everything to do with the exchange those two great men had that day. The president and the pope were allies in the battle against Soviet-style communism. Neither saw that battle as merely political. To both it was an existential struggle over the truth of the human person.[10]

For John Paul II particularly, the great evil of communism was the materialism that lay at its heart. Communism denied God. It denied the transcendent. It saw only the things of the world, and it valued only what it could see. Accordingly, it was an ideology that equated "having more" with being more, and its proponents committed any number of atrocities, denied any number of freedoms, and violated any number of rights in their purported efforts to secure the greatest amount of material happiness for the greatest number of people.

John Paul II understood the evils of communism from the inside out. He lived for three decades—from priest to cardinal—under Communist rule in Poland. But his opposition to the Soviet Union wasn't rooted in his personal experiences of Communist atrocities. It was rooted in what he believed to be true, right, and good. His opposition was ethical more than it was personal. His understanding of ethics, of what was right and what was wrong, gave him the clarity of vision and strength of conviction to stand firm against communism.

Despite constant threats, despite the 1981 assassination attempt that many believed was ordered by the KGB, and despite all the pressure on him to stand down and stop speaking out against communism, John Paul II persisted publicly and privately in his opposition to the totalitarian system. Where personal emotion or more visceral animosity could have clouded his vision and hindered his judgment, a clear ethical framework did just the opposite.

Just two years after the pope and the president's 1987 meeting, the Berlin Wall did indeed fall. Everyone involved in the struggle, from the president of the United States to the first democratically elected presidents in the Eastern Bloc, credited the pope's clear moral vision as one of the primary reasons why.

Competing Ethical Frameworks:
Utilitarianism vs. Person Centeredness

More than two decades have passed since the Soviet Union collapsed. While Russia today is hardly a beacon of democracy, the existential struggle in which John Paul II and Reagan were engaged seems to be over. But is it?

In many ways, the materialist mindset the pope combated continues to this day in the forms of Western relativism and consumerism. Both, like communism, deny the transcendent. Both equate "having" with "being" and deny absolute truth. The fruits of modern materialism are evident in every aspect of Western life, from the breakdown of the family to the abysmal state of education. They are also evident in the way we do business.

One need look no further than the economic collapse which followed the sub-prime mortgage crisis in late 2008 for evidence. The financial ruin of millions didn't happen because of one person or one company's wrong doing. It happened because countless individuals, from powerful CEOs and politicians to low-level mortgage brokers and real estate speculators, placed financial gain over acting rightly and justly. They didn't act alone. In their efforts, they were helped by millions of consumers who shared their values.

Those values weren't formed overnight. They were formed slowly, by years of seemingly inconsequential decisions and habits, the sort of decisions to which it's easy to turn a blind eye. A little number fudging here, a little expense account padding there—that's where it begins. By the time the big ethical dilemma actually presents itself, it's too late. Your response has been all but predetermined by the thousands of little choices you've made through the years.

That's why it's so important to approach both life and work as John Paul II did, with a clear moral framework, a system of ethics that can serve as a compass, consistently pointing you in the right direction regardless of what circumstances or challenges you face.

That system of ethics needs to be based on more than what the culture believes is right at any given point in time. It also needs to be based on more than what the law says is right at any given point in time. Neither are ever enough. Both can change. Both can be wrong. Both can crumble when tested.

Again, look at the sub-prime crisis. Much of what went on was legal. The products mortgage companies offered were designed to fall ever so slightly on the right side of the law. But were those products moral? Was creating them, offering them, and buying them the ethical thing to do? Only if your guiding ethic is short-term financial profit at any cost.

If you want to lead your team honestly, justly, and, in the long run, successfully, something more is needed than knowledge of the law. You need a true standard by which to evaluate all the day-to-day decisions you make. You need a clear and consistent framework that is in accord with the truth about man, the world, and God. That is a framework that John Paul II proposed. It is a framework derived from John's first letter: "Beloved, let us love one another, because love is of God; everyone who loves is begotten by God and knows God. Whoever is without love does not know God, for God is love" (1 John 4:7–8).

The Problem of Utilitarianism: Self-Centered Ethics

Before we define what John Paul's proposed framework is, however, it's helpful to first define its opposite: utilitarianism. Whether they know it or not, many people today abide by a utilitarian ethical framework. They consider pleasure in this life the highest end that man can attain, and they believe that securing the maximum amount of pleasure for the greatest possible number of people is the goal of political, economic, and social activity. If the happiness or even lives of a few people must be sacrificed in order to obtain that pleasure for the greater number of men, that's okay according to the utilitarian framework. If one person needs to be used by another for the sake of pleasure, that's okay too.

Utilitarianism is the ethical framework behind pornography. It tells me it's okay to treat another person as an object and ask them to do things that will harm them physically, emotionally, and spiritually, so that I can obtain sexual enjoyment.

Utilitarianism is also the ethical framework behind pollution. It sanctions my company's decision to not put mechanisms in place that will prevent toxic chemicals from entering the ground water or poisonous particulates from going into the air because doing so would impact our profit margin.

Utilitarianism is what allows CEOs to justify firing hardworking employees while top management uses the company jet for personal travel, and it's what allows corporate executives to collect giant bonuses while short-changing shareholders. It's what makes marketing executives feel comfortable convincing people to spend more than they have, and it's why many corporate cultures become so tolerant of violations of moral rules (such as lying about a product's abilities or an investment's risks) among its employees. Everything and everyone is seen through the lens of short-term financial profit and pleasure. Everything and everyone is, in effect, a means or measure of pleasure.

John Paul's Proposed Ethical Framework: Person-Centered Ethics

That's not how it's supposed to be. The human person is made in the image and likeness of God. We are the crown of creation and destined to become a partaker of the Divine Nature, to be God's adopted children living in his presence for all eternity. We all have a shot at an end that is far more glorious than the mere experience of pleasure.

Because of that, a person can never be an object. He can never be used as a means to an end. A person can choose to sacrifice himself for the greater good. A soldier can die for his country, a mother can go without food so that her child might eat, but no one can make that sacrifice for them. No one can force it upon them. Instead, John Paul declared "the person is the kind of good toward which the only proper and adequate attitude is love."[11]

Those truths are at the heart of John Paul II's framework.[12] John Paul II lived according to an ethical framework that places the human person at the center of all activity. The extent to which the good of the human person was furthered was the measure by which he judged ideas and actions. Likewise love, not the desire to maximize pleasure, was the attitude he believed should motivate all actions.

John Paul II made no secret of this ethical framework. It was evident in the two philosophical books he published before becoming pope, *The Acting Person* and *Love and Responsibility*. It was also evident in his first encyclical, "The Redeemer of Man," and just about everything he wrote afterwards. In that first encyclical, John Paul introduced a theme that would resound throughout his papacy. There, he wrote:

> Does this progress, which has man for its author and promoter, make human life on earth 'more human' in every aspect of that life?…What is most essential—whether in the context of this progress man, as man, is becoming truly better, that is to say more mature spiritually, more aware of the dignity of his humanity, more responsible, more open to others, especially the neediest and weakest, and readier to give and to aid all.[13]

That's the framework in a nutshell, and that is why John Paul II so steadfastly opposed communism. In communism, the good of the person is secondary to the good of the collective. In Communist societies, individuals haven't been loved by those who rule them;

they've been used. Their ultimate good is never considered. Who they are, who God made them to be, their own desires and hopes—none of those things are taken into consideration by the Communist system. Communism makes men less human, not more.

That also is why John Paul II spoke out against forms of capitalism that weren't underpinned by a Judeo-Christian ethic of charity, honesty, and personal responsibility. He saw in the forerunners of corrupt mortgage lenders and Enron executives the same utilitarian ethic that turned the wheels of communism.

Above all, that person-centered ethic is why John Paul was such a staunch defender of attacks against the dignity of the human person—abortion, contraception, euthanasia, and the diminishment of the family. He saw all those things and countless other political and social movements demeaning men, making them less than what they were. He also saw people using other people, seeking pleasure at any cost. He knew how fundamentally destructive those behaviors were.

This was evident in his remarks to the Vatican Diplomatic Corps on January 13, 2003. On that day, he repeated a thought he had said many times before:

> Respect life itself and individual lives: everything starts
> here, for the most fundamental of human rights is certainly
> the right to life. Abortion, euthanasia, human cloning, for
> example, risk reducing the human person to a mere object:
> life and death to order, as it were![14]

Whenever a new controversy or question arose, John Paul II had the good of the human person as his measuring stick, his tool by which to evaluate and judge a thing's worth. That measuring stick was his constant, an unchanging ethic rooted in divinely revealed truth. He didn't need the government to tell him it was right to oppose abortion. He didn't need the culture to tell him he should help the Church open AIDS hospices throughout Africa.

He had a guiding principle; an ethical framework , that unfailingly guided him, helping him know the difference between right and wrong.

Others saw that, including President Reagan. That's why he considered John Paul II his most valuable ally in the fight against communism and why he made a point of meeting with him before dramatically calling for the toppling of the Berlin Wall. The Communists saw it as well. That's why they did everything they could to minimize the pope and silence him. All of us who served the man, who watched him day in and day out, weathering storms of controversy and public scorn, saw it too.

Leading According to a Person-Centered Ethic

John Paul's person-centered ethic is just as applicable to leading a company as it is to leading the Church. When properly understood, it gives you the very tool you need to steer your team or company straight and true through the moral maze of the market.

That understanding starts with recognizing that all economic activity is undertaken because of human beings. Not in the abstract, but specifically and individually. A company exists for two reasons: to satisfy the needs of its customers and to enable its employees and investors to earn a living while using their God-given gifts and talents in service to others. These individuals are at the center of every business and every business activity. Decisions made with a person-centered ethic lead you to an end where both the good of the customers and the good of the employees are achieved.

The key word there is "both." It's never enough for a company to serve its customers at the cost of its employees' health and well-being or vice-versa. The good of both must be secured.

Rightly Ordered Objectives

To illustrate this "both/and" concept, it might be helpful to briefly consider the Church's teachings on marriage. In the Catholic tradition, marriage is considered the ultimate human relationship, a relationship modeled on the life and love of the Trinity and therefore a model, in many ways, for all other human relationships, business relationships included.

Marriage's first objective is procreation—the propagation of the human race through bearing children and raising them in a stable, loving environment. Its second aim is mutual support—to give two people the benefit of another's help and advice so that they might grow in wisdom and love. The third aim is the fulfillment of the desire of the spouses, the psychological and physical joy that loving and being loved can produce.

None of those aims can be realized at the expense of the other. If a man enters marriage solely to satisfy his physical desires and has no intent of being a support to his wife or being open to children, he's acting unethically. He's violating the person-centered ethic (i.e., he uses another person for his own good or, more to the point, not for their joint good).

The same goes for all other relationships. All healthy human relationships, in some way, should be life-giving, should provide mutual support, and should be psychologically or physically beneficial to the participants.

When it comes to business specifically, those general objectives take on a concrete form.

1. A business is life-giving when a group of individuals participate in God's creative power, working together to pursue a common good by giving life to an idea, product, or service. This norm is what makes work spiritually fulfilling. It's violated when the idea, product, or service destroys life literally (e.g., suicide machines, dangerous drugs, etc.) or destroys life spiritually, either for individuals or cultures (e.g., pornography).

2. A business provides mutual support when it effectively fulfills legitimate customer needs at a competitive price. By "legitimate" I mean moral, a need that doesn't contribute in any way to harming a person physically or spiritually.

3. A business benefits its employees and owners, psychologically and physically, when it generates enough profit to sustain a reasonable system of financial rewards (wages and shareholder return). This is important both for attracting good employees who uphold the quality of the business and for maintaining its investors.

Violate any one of those objectives and your business will fail to thrive. Ignore the person at the center of the activity, ignore the team or stifle creativity, and the business suffers. Ignore legitimate customer needs and manufacture products that are destructive or useless, and the business dies. Ignore giving reasonable financial rewards and incentives to the participants in the business and ignore giving share values or profits to the shareholders, and the business becomes unsustainable.

What's true in human relationships is true in business relationships. The good of the person always has to come first. It has to be the guide, shaping your decisions, policies, and practices. It has to form the foundation of your professional and personal ethic. Only when it does can your business and everything else in your life flourish.

***

In 1988, shortly after the pope returned from a visit to Berlin, I was standing guard outside his private apartment when the future Pope Benedict XVI, Cardinal Joseph Ratzinger, stopped by for a visit. The cardinal had been with the pope in Berlin, where less than friendly crowds greeted them. Activists staged huge protests and launched eggs and tomatoes at the "popemobile" as it drove by.

While Cardinal Ratzinger waited for admittance to the rooms, I began to chat with him. He's a gentle man, shy but friendly and sincere. That particular day I was curious about the reception Berlin had given the two and asked what it was like to be attacked as they had been.

"Doesn't it bother you to have eggs and tomatoes thrown at you? Doesn't it hurt your feelings?" I asked.

He smiled in his gentle way and explained, "No, because what they're throwing they're not throwing at Karol Wojtyla and Joseph Ratzinger. If the two of us had never been involved in Christ's message, they wouldn't be throwing anything at us. The tomatoes and insults are intended for what we stand for and what we proclaim. It is the Christian faith which has been handed down to us through the centuries. We can't change that because it is difficult to live up to or doesn't fit the current cultural trends. We should proclaim it in love, but it's not ours to change."

How the cardinal saw the situation was how John Paul II saw it. Christ had given them a message—the Good News. Reason had given them an ethical framework for incarnating that message in their day-to-day decisions—the person-centered ethic. They could only be truly successful if they were faithful to that, if they held true to what they had been given and upheld the ultimate dignity of the human person regardless of the cost. In their fidelity to what is right, what is true, they found their strength.

Meeting the Right Objectives

Wonder if your business is meeting its primary objectives for all parties involved? Answer the questions below and find out.

Objectives
1. **Creativity:**
   How is my company's work life-giving and creative? How is it helping everyone involved not just make more but also become more?

   What are ways to improve?

2. Support:

How does our work support the needs of everyone involved?
Are these needs legitimate?

What are ways to improve?

3. Benefit:

How is our work physically and/or psychologically beneficial
to all participants? Is it financially sustainable for all involved?

What are ways to improve?

Questions for Reflection

1. Have you seen utilitarianism at work in your business or
   profession? How has that impacted the individuals involved,
   both customers and employees?

2. Draw or describe your ethical framework. How do you
   evaluate right from wrong? To what or whom do you turn
   when you find yourself in "gray areas"? How did you come by
   this framework?

3. Think of a situation at work where you, your manager, or
   an employee let utilitarianism be the guiding principle? How
   would the situation have turned out differently if a person-
   centered ethic had been used?

4. What are five principles of person-centered ethics that you can
   apply to your work every day?

Chapter Four

Know How to Choose What's Right:
Exercising Your Free Will

Sometimes a way seems right to a man, but the end of it leads to death!

Proverbs 14:12

In [the act of entrusting oneself to God], the intellect and the will display their spiritual nature, enabling the subject to act in a way which realizes personal freedom to the full. It is not just that freedom is part of the act of faith: it is absolutely required. Indeed, it is faith that allows individuals to give consummate expression to their own freedom. Put differently, freedom is not realized in decisions made against God. For how could it be an exercise of true freedom to refuse to be open to the very reality that enables our self-realization?

—Blessed John Paul II

In April 1987, the Swiss Guards at the Vatican were anxiously awaiting John Paul II's return to Rome. He had just spent several weeks visiting Latin America, where he was only grudgingly welcomed. The people were thrilled to see him. It was their governments who were being difficult. With them, his firm opposition to their repeated human rights violations made him less than popular.

In Chile things got particularly bad, with the government staging a riot at one of the pope's large, outdoor Masses. The other guards and I had seen some coverage of the events on the news, but we wanted the full story from our friends who witnessed it on the ground.

When we got that story it was far worse and far more inspiring than the news coverage had led us to believe. Apparently, the riots

---

Epigraph. Encyclical letter on the relationship between Faith and Reason *Fides et Ratio* (November 2000), 13.

in Chile were sparked by government officials who were present at the outdoor Mass. When the pope began praying the Sacred Liturgy, they launched into a nationalistic anthem. Singing at the tops of their lungs, they attempted to drown out his voice. When the Catholic faithful in attendance tried to silence them, the military responded by aiming tear gas into the crowds.

Amidst the pandemonium, the altar remained peaceful. Most men in John Paul's position would have grown angry or retired to safety, but he took a different course. When the officials shouted out their songs, he prayed a little louder. He continued to pray when the rioting broke out. With tear gas in the air, he prayed more still. He didn't shout, and he didn't run. He made the decision that celebrating that Mass, despite all the forces arrayed against him, was the most important thing he could do for God and the Chilean people. He knew he needed to show them that the government could not silence the Church. It could not silence God.

John Paul focused on the task at hand and chose to respond in the way he believed God wanted him to respond. He was able to do that not simply because he knew it was the right thing to do, but also, more importantly, because over a period of many years, he had made a habit of choosing the right course of action. He had learned to discipline his will to choose the good, even when that choice was difficult. He had, in fact, learned to use his free will rightly.

The Challenge of Free Will

In life, ethics can only get you so far. There is, after all, a difference between knowing what's right and doing what's right. A solid ethical framework can help you with the former, but with the latter, something more is needed. That something is the ability to exercise your free will in service of the good, to consciously choose the correct course of action regardless of the obstacles and temptations standing in your way.

That ability is something all of us can cultivate. Simply by virtue of being human, we all possess the power to make good choices. That's what free will gives you—the ability to exercise control over how you conduct yourself in public and in private, as well as over what you choose to believe. Whether you run your business honestly or dishonestly, whether you remain faithful to your spouse or commit adultery, whether you give your life to God or reject his loving mercy—all those things are choices that hinge upon the right exercise of your free will.

In many ways, free will is what gives your life meaning. Without it, your good actions and bad actions would have no value because they would not really be your actions, freely chosen. There could be no such thing as sin without free will, because sin involves both the recognition that a certain action is wrong and the choice to engage in that action regardless. Likewise, there could be no such thing as virtue, because virtue requires the conscious choice to act rightly. Free will is what makes it possible for you to become a sinner or a saint.

It's important to note, however, that the power to choose for yourself what is good, doesn't mean all choices are, in fact, good. There are good choices and bad choices. The good choices are choices made in conformity with God's will. The bad choices violate God's will. Free will is only exercised rightly when it brings your actions and your will into accord with God's perfect will. That's the goal. That's the end for which you should strive to use your free will.

Free Will as the Key to Successful Leadership
John Paul II was able to choose the correct action in the midst of a Chilean riot because he had already spent a lifetime training his will, exercising it in small matters and in great matters in the service of the good. His right responses were, at that point, second nature, a virtuous habit formed over the course of decades.

That habit is one reason why he served God and led the Catholic Church so successfully. He knew how to choose the right course of action and follow that choice through. He didn't get distracted by matters of secondary importance and could focus on what mattered most at any given point in time. Moreover, by his example of right action, he taught those serving under him to respond rightly too.

That same habit is just as crucial for an executive or CEO. You can't be successful without having a will disciplined enough to help you achieve your goals. You can't lead your company to success without having the ability to pursue the right course of action. You can't create a corporate culture of responsibility and innovation unless you've modeled those behaviors for your employees.

You can't allow yourself to become distracted, unfocused, or lazy as the person ultimately responsible for your business' future. You have to be willing to do the hard work and make the hard choices, and you actually have to do both. If you don't, nobody else will.

Over the years, I've worked with plenty of CEOs and managers who don't think those rules apply to them. They think they hit a certain point in their careers where the hard work stops, and they can just coast on the record of their past successes. These are the managers who stop coming to meetings and answering their employees' questions, who secure perks for themselves that nobody else has, who take salaries dramatically out of proportion to their actual contributions to the company. These are also the CEOs who appoint their buddies to the board so they don't have to face strict scrutiny over their decisions and the company's numbers. They pad and fiddle with the bottom line, acting increasingly disingenuous as the years pass.

It may not happen overnight, but in the long run, the company always suffers for that kind of behavior. When the person at the helm doesn't have the strength of will to work hard and work honestly, he and everyone whose livelihoods depend upon him get blown off course. They don't accomplish what they set out to accomplish. The vision, once shared, dies.

That's why free will matters, in business and in life. That's why nobody who wants to lead well can put off until tomorrow the work of training their will. By tomorrow, it may already be too late.

God's Authority and Will

In the years before and after he became pope, John Paul II was sought out by innumerable friends and students for advice and spiritual direction. They would come to him with a problem, expecting he would tell them what to do. But it rarely worked that way. Sometimes he would ask them questions. Other times, he would ask them to take some time to think things over. Through all that talking and thinking, he wanted them to come to see for themselves the various sides of a question or what was at stake. Once they did, he still didn't tell them what to do. "You must make the decision," was what he would always say.

What John Paul wanted for those advice seekers was that they exercise their free will. In that, he purposefully imitated God, although many people today don't recognize that.

John Paul often lamented that people didn't understand the gift of their free will or the nature of God's authority. The fact that the right exercise of free will means choosing God's way, not our own, both confuses and frustrates many. They see that as a denial of their freedom, a restriction on their liberty. They also see God not as a loving Father, but as a repressive and authoritarian dictator, asking them to do what they don't want to do.

In that, many seem to confuse their heavenly Father with their earthly fathers or other authority figures they've known. That's easy enough to understand. All of us, at some point or other, have suffered under the arbitrary rule of someone misusing their authority—a parent, a teacher, a boss, a commanding officer. We've been repressed, judged, limited, shamed, and abandoned at their direction. The more times that happens, the less willing we are to trust anyone with authority. We see an adversarial system at work in the world—oppressor and oppressed—and we assume that same system is at work in the Church, with God being the oppressor and us being the oppressed.

A True Father

If that were how God operated, we would be more than justified in not trusting him. But that's not how things work. God doesn't wield authority like a power-hungry dictator. He doesn't want to oppress you or force you to do his will. He doesn't want to force you to do anything. That's where free will comes in. God wants you to choose for yourself what you will believe and not believe, what you will do and not do. He wants you to choose willingly and joyfully what he asks of you.

What he asks of you is never arbitrary and never wrong. It may be difficult. It may go against what you instinctively desire for yourself or what the culture at large says that you should want, but it nevertheless is good for you. It's what will lead you to true happiness and eternal life.

That's how God's law always works. It's a roadmap for happiness based upon how God made you. You were made to want certain things and do certain things and only when you pursue them can you find joy. Only when you live according to God's will, do you discover who you truly are and find the grace to be truly free. In God, you don't lose yourself, you find yourself.[15]

That's why, although God wants you to choose for yourself what you will believe and do, there are still right choices and wrong choices, good ones and bad ones. That's also why there are consequences for choosing wrongly.

When you choose not to live in accord with truth, and how you were made, things will go wrong. It's like using the wrong tool for a construction job. You're not going to get the outcome you want. There will be problems. Those problems, however, are your doing, not God's. You're suffering at your own hands, not his. Sin brings its own punishment, and eventually, whether it takes us a day, a month, or a lifetime, we all come to see the truth of that.

If you want to be happy and successful, if you want to live and act rightly, making the correct choices and taking the correct actions, you have to let go of any fears and hang-ups about God's authority and will, and do everything you can to bring your will into conformity with his. You have to practice, like a great athlete would, seeking out every occasion to strengthen your will. I learned as a Swiss Guard that such practice must happen both in thought and in deed.

Training the Will: Learning to Stand Still

Swiss Guards are probably most famous for the statue-like stance they take outside the pope's palace. Tourists almost make a game of trying to get the sentinel on duty to look at them or smile. Women wink, blow kisses, and make all sorts of proposals. Men do gymnastics, crack jokes, or even throw an insult or two at the guard, hoping to get a rise of out him.

It never happens. The sentinel doesn't really notice their antics. It's not his job to notice them, or, for that matter, anything else going on around him. Sentinel duty is just an honor guard duty. It's a sign of respect the Vatican pays to visitors. The real work is done by a more senior guard who stands nearby. While he controls crowds and helps out tourists, the sentinel just has to stand still. He has to do that for a very, very long time. Trust me, that is work. There are two tricks that help.

The Habit of Right-Thinking

The first trick has to do with your attitude or the thoughts on which you allow your mind to dwell.

The older guards always told us that doing sentinel duty reluctantly or grudgingly makes the action twice as hard. They were right. That's because when you resent something, your resentment becomes the focus of your thoughts. You dwell on it, ruminate on it, and every little thing that's difficult about what you're doing is magnified. If, on the other hand, your attitude is positive, if you willingly embrace what you've been asked or, in the Swiss Guard's case, ordered to do, your mind doesn't dwell on the duty. It goes elsewhere to contemplate more pleasant thoughts.

What's true for Swiss Guards on sentinel duty is true for everyone. Thoughts matter. The thoughts we think, the thoughts on which we permit our minds to dwell, contribute to both the right and wrong exercise of our free will. They are the first step in the choices we make, and they can lead us in good directions or bad ones.

Long ago, the early desert fathers and mothers—the forerunners of Western monks and cloistered religious—actually worked up a system to classify human thoughts. They asserted that all the thoughts or "demons" with which a desert hermit had to contend could be broken down into eight general categories: gluttony, lust, avarice, anger, sadness, sloth, vainglory, and pride. In everyday language, that's food, sex, possessions, anger, depression, indifference, your reputation, and your ego.

That list sounds negative, but that's not necessarily the case. Depending on your response, the desert fathers believed those thoughts could actually lead you toward the good. All those long solitary hours in the wilderness taught them that while they couldn't necessarily control what thoughts assailed them, they could control their reaction to them. They could choose to dwell on them, thereby moving one step closer to acting on them. Or they could choose to reject them. The way to reject them was to focus on something else, something better, something that could become the first step toward virtue or right action.

In order to perform sentinel duty, that was a habit I had to master. I had to learn to not focus on thoughts of resentment or annoyance, and instead think about better things: the tradition of which I was a part, my life and the decisions I'd made up to that point, where I was going, and what I wanted to do in the years ahead. By using sentinel duty to think about those things, it became not only bearable, but an important part of my conversion to deeper faith in Christ and his Church.

The habit of controlling my thoughts is a habit I still need to cultivate. I can't allow my thoughts to lead me (and subsequently my company) in the wrong direction.

That's what happens when executives start to entertain the temptations to power, greed, dishonesty, sexual immorality, callousness, and other destructive behaviors that inevitably come their way. Those thoughts become the seeds of bad actions.

All bad choices start out as thoughts: "The rules don't apply to me." "I'm better than others." "Nobody will know if I cover up this mistake." "That person is expendable." The thoughts are almost inescapable. What's not inescapable is entertaining those thoughts. You can choose not to dwell on them. You can choose to focus on something else: your commitments to God, your family, and your employees; your desire to be creative and innovative; the needs you can meet and the people you can serve; your own dependence on God's grace, mercy, and love.

For every negative thought that enters your head, there is a countervailing positive thought. When you focus on those, you lay the groundwork for right action. You encourage your will to move in the direction of the good and the true. In effect, you nourish your will with what it needs to choose rightly.

You don't, however, have to wait until a bad thought comes along to focus on a good thought. You can, in fact, create good thoughts by seeking out something good or important on which to dwell and starting a train of thought that can lead to good actions.

One of the ways John Paul II did this was to work on his will every year on his birthday.[16] He would review the events of his life and the past year, contemplate what he would like to see in the year ahead, and pray about what he wanted his legacy to be. Every year, in a focused, disciplined way, he examined the whole of his life, past, present, and future. That process and the thoughts that emerged from it, helped him pursue his goals with deepened passion and vigor.

That's something we all can do on a personal level. We can also do it on a professional level. Having more than a one or two-year business or career plan is essential. Thinking about what you want, five, ten, even twenty years down the road, is the first step in actually reaching those goals. They are thoughts that feed the will and help you to make choices that will lead you where you want to go.

Practice Makes Perfect

Earlier, I wrote that two things helped me develop the discipline and peace of mind to endure the seemingly endless hours of standing still outside the papal palace. The first was learning to control my thoughts. What was the second?

The second was the exact posture I adopted at the beginning of each round of sentinel duty. The position you adopted at the outset had everything to do with how long you could endure remaining motionless. If you adopted the right one, your joints and bones settled into a state of skeletal balance, where everything rested just as it should and your body stood almost by itself. That level of physical comfort made the task mentally easier. You weren't sore, stiff, or in pain, so your thoughts tended to move on a higher plane. If, however, you adopted the wrong position, your body could never manage to rest rightly and doing your duty became a near impossibility. Your thoughts never strayed far from your discomfort and refocusing them was a serious challenge.

The virtuous exercise of the free will is much like sentinel duty in that respect. Your body influences your mind. Thoughts may precede actions, but actions can also precede thoughts. Kneeling to pray can make you feel more prayerful. Working in a quiet room, away from the television, can make you feel more interested in the task at hand. Writing a large check to charity can make you enjoy giving more. When you first undertake any of those actions—kneeling, working, or practicing generosity—you may not be feeling particularly prayerful, diligent, or generous. The feelings are secondary. What matters is the action. Quite often, the feelings follow the action. Merely starting an activity will bring about the required frame of mind.

Similarly, like with sentinel duty, small decisions early on (such as what posture you adopt) shape your ability to choose what's right later down the road. In a sense, your will settles into a certain position.

In other words, the morality or immorality of your actions in the present have a lot to do with how you've used your free will in the past. The more you use it to choose moral actions, the stronger it grows and the easier it becomes to continually choose moral actions. The more you use it to choose immoral actions, the weaker it grows and the harder it becomes to choose moral actions.

In many ways, free will is like a muscle. It needs to be trained and strengthened in order for it to work properly. It needs to be disciplined. If not used well, it atrophies. Through the repeated right exercise of it in small things—honoring a daily commitment to prayer, keeping promises to your spouse and children, meeting deadlines at the office—it grows stronger.

It grows stronger still when you forego small comforts and pleasures in order to cultivate the habit of self-denial. Passing up dessert, getting up as soon as your alarm goes off, and not watching television on weeknights are all little acts of sacrifice that bring the will under the control of the intellect. The more you practice consciously choosing what's good but difficult in small matters, the easier it becomes to choose the good but difficult in large matters.

**

When I first arrived at the Vatican and observed the senior guards doing things such as walking in lockstep or throwing the halberd—a long pole capped with an axe—I was in awe. They performed every movement, every motion with mind-boggling precision.

I'll never forget the first time I saw my instructor, Martino, throw the halberd. While standing at attention, he tossed it high into the air, and then caught it at an exact point marked by a nail. Next he pulled it close into his body with one arm, and guided it to his shoulder with the other. Then it smacked back down to the floor, exactly to the edge of his shoes, without hitting his toes. He did it with such ease and grace, almost without effort. Or so it seemed.

"No way will I ever be able to do that," I remember thinking. "It's impossible."

But it wasn't. After hours and hours of throwing and catching (and hitting my toes with the bottom of the halbard), I could do it with as much ease and precision as Martino. I could also march in lock step, jump to attention, and do all the other guard duties that at first seemed so very foreign. With enough hard work and practice, they became second nature to me too.

That's also how it works with free will. Choosing the good as easily, confidently, and consistently as John Paul II did can seem all but impossible at times. The more you practice and the harder you work, the easier it becomes. With that ease comes peace, joy, and the ability to do all that God has set out for you. With it comes the ability to become the man or woman he created you to be.

Words of Wisdom on the Will

Just as Christ once came on earth in the flesh to accomplish our salvation, so He comes daily in the spirit to save each individual soul; the difference is that His first coming was visible to the eye, whereas the second is unseen. As scripture says: Christ the Lord is the breath of life to us, and the hidden nature of this spiritual coming is shown in the continuation of the same text: Under His shadow we shall live among the nations.

70

For this reason, even if you are too sick to go very far to meet the Lord, it is appropriate for you to respond to the great physician's visit by making an effort at least to raise your head and lift yourself up a little to greet Him on his arrival.

—St. Bernard of Clairvaux

Questions for Reflection

1. Describe your own experience with authority figures—your parents, teachers, employers, etc. How has it been positive and negative? What has resulted from obeying those in authority? Has that had an impact on the way you understand God's authority? What are three ideas from your past experience with your own, human authority figures that you affix as attributes to God?

2. Virtues are really nothing more than good habits, or, said in a different way: the habituation of good judgment. We acquire them through repeated right actions. Vices are virtue's opposite, bad habits acquired through repeated wrong actions. List three virtues (or good habits) and three vices (or bad habits) you've developed over the years. How do those virtues and vices affect your work life? Your home life?

3. List five small sacrifices you can incorporate into your everyday life to retrain your will and overcome those vices listed above? What are five small actions you can take to magnify your virtues? What difference will that make at work? At home?

Chapter Five

Know Where You Are and Where You Are Going:
Bridging the Paradox of Planning for the Future yet Living in the Present

I know the plans I have for you, declares the Lord, plans to prosper you and not to harm you, plans to give you hope and a future.

Jeremiah 29:11 NIV

"Do not worry about tomorrow; tomorrow will take care of itself. Sufficient for a day is its own evil."

Matthew 6:34

To all men and women without exception, I wish to ask them to be convinced of the seriousness of the present moment and of each one's individual responsibility, and to implement—by the way they live as individuals and as families, by the use of their resources, by their civic activity, by contributing to economic and political decisions and by personal commitment to national and international undertakings—the measures inspired by solidarity and love of preference for the poor.

—Blessed John Paul II

On Christmas Eve, 1986, I was one of the saddest Swiss Guards in the papal palace. Bad enough it was my first Christmas away from home, but because of the assignment I'd drawn—guarding the anteroom of the pope's private apartments in the hours before Midnight Mass—I wouldn't even be able to celebrate Christmas with the other guards.

All afternoon, my thoughts were with my family in Switzerland. Christmas Eve was always our favorite holiday, and in my head I could almost smell my mother's roast cooking and see my father decorating our tree. I could hear the carols in the background and imagine the conversations taking place between my siblings. As

---

Epigraph. Encyclical Letter for the twentieth anniversary of "Populorum Progressio" *Sollicitudo Rei Socialis* (December 20, 1987), 47.

the youngest of six children, I'd never been away from home for any extended period of time, let alone on Christmas, and as the afternoon wore on, my depression grew. I was the "newbie" in the Guards that Christmas, having only arrived weeks before, and was trying hard to hide my struggle, to play it cool. I really wasn't sure how long the act could hold.

Shortly before I went on duty, I got in line with the other guards to make our calls home. When it was my turn, I spoke to my father first. I did pretty well with him. My voice didn't crack and my face was expressionless. I was keenly aware that there was a line of men standing behind me, watching and listening in.

Then my father put my mother on the phone. I didn't stand a chance.

She was crying because her "baby" wasn't home for Christmas. I don't know about you, but when my mother cries, I have to cry with her. I fought it as much as I could and did my best to hide it, but the tears came regardless. I hung up the phone and ran to my room, put on my uniform, and headed out for my solitary Christmas Eve guarding the papal apartments. It was dark and lonely up there, and there was nothing to do. That meant I had plenty of time to mull over my sadness and think about my family celebrating Christmas without me. I missed them terribly, and as the hours passed I worked myself into a miserable state.

At about ten o'clock that evening, I got a call on my radio. An officer informed me that John Paul was leaving to celebrate Midnight Mass and would use my exit. I had just enough time to straighten my uniform before the door opened. A warm light from the apartment flooded my dark post. Then the pope came out. With the backlight and his splendid white robe, he looked like a heavenly vision.

As he came out, he paused about twenty feet from me. He looked at me for some time without saying anything. Then he spoke.

"You're new! What's your name?" he asked.

I told him and he came closer, peering into my reddened eyes. He immediately understood what was going on and said, "This is your first Christmas away from home, isn't it?"

I replied in the affirmative, barely holding back tears as I answered.

Yet again, he stepped closer, pausing just inches from me this time. Taking my hand with one hand and holding my elbow with the other, he pulled me slightly toward him, looked at me with his deep gray eyes, and said, "Andreas, I want to thank you for the sacrifice you are making for the Church. I will pray for you during Mass this evening."

That was all I needed. Someone had noticed my pain, someone had cared, and that someone was the pope himself. In the moment, I felt comforted. Now, looking back, I feel amazed. Here was the leader of a billion Catholics, at the height of some of his fiercest battles, occupied with the most overwhelming and impossible problems of the century, yet he was still sensitive enough to perceive the emotions of a twenty-year-old guard whose sole job was to blend into the background as he passed. Our roles should have been reversed—with me observing him—but they weren't.

Continually, John Paul II somehow managed to find the balance between pursuing a vision that impacted billions and being completely in the moment every day and everywhere. He saw both the big picture and the little picture, never losing sight of the importance of either one.

As it does for every leader, that made all the difference.

Know Where You Are

A strong leader always knows where he's going. He sees ahead. Like John Paul II, he also needs to know where he is. He needs to see what's right in front of him.

It continues to amaze me that in my meeting with him on that Christmas Eve in 1986—at the height of the Cold War, a time when he had millions of reasons to be preoccupied and absorbed in far more important matters—the pope noticed me. It was rather like a person noticing a chirping grasshopper in the middle of a bustling city.

It was always like that with John Paul II. Whenever I encountered the pope, it unfailingly felt as if I was the reason he got up in the morning. He was always fully present, keenly aware of what was going on in the heart and mind of the person to whom he spoke and far more interested in what you had to say to him than what he had to say to you. No matter what other pressing concerns awaited him at the end of your conversation, those concerns were seemingly absent from his mind while he was with you.

He was able to do that, in part, because of his vision. The fact that he had a well thought out plan of action, that he contemplated and prayed about his mission down to the smallest details, gave him the freedom and serenity he needed to live fully in the moment.

Conversely, the only way he was able to realize his vision is because he knew how to be present in the moment. He understood the human person—with all his hopes, desires, and struggles—not because he read about the human person in a book, but because he knew specific human persons, deeply and intimately. He knew how the contemporary culture was damaging people, not because of newspaper stories, but because of the stories individuals brought to him on a daily basis.

Likewise, his vision inspired those of us who helped him realize it, not just because it was a good vision, but because he was a good man, a man who we knew cared deeply about us and the world. He was attentive to us in the small things, and so we were all the more willing to help him out in the big things.

One story that illustrates this was told to me by a fellow Swiss Guard, Bernard. One sweltering summer day, he stood guard at the summer residence, Castel Gandolfo, which is just outside Rome. He was in the center of the courtyard, dripping with sweat thanks to his heavy uniform and the hot Italian sun, when the pope and a few colleagues emerged from one door and walked directly into another. They never stepped out into the courtyard, just skirted around its edges as they walked from one door to the next. Bernard saluted them, but doubted at the time that they saw him.

He, however, was wrong in the case of John Paul II. Just moments after the pope disappeared behind the door, one of the religious sisters who worked with him came into the courtyard with a pitcher of water. John Paul II thought Bernard might be thirsty, standing in the hot sun, and requested the water be sent out.

John Paul II never failed to see those in front of him. People were never less important to him than his immediate tasks or long-term goals. That's why his presence in the moment wasn't just one of attentiveness, but also of understanding.

John Paul II recognized the struggles he faced in the immediate situation. He was keenly aware of people's resentment toward the Church, of the wounds some of his predecessors and other sons and daughters of the Church had inflicted in the past. He didn't run from those wounds or ignore them. He recognized them, took responsibility for them, and apologized for them.

To mark the Great Jubilee Year of 2000 and prepare the way for the Church into the twenty-first century, John Paul II offered a formal apology to the world for sins committed by members of the Church and by all Christians over the centuries. It was in that spirit that he journeyed to Israel to pay homage to the victims of the Holocaust. He was also the first pope ever to enter a mosque, and the first to visit Greece and the Orthodox Patriarch since the Eastern Church split from the West twelve hundred years prior.

Some criticized those efforts. They thought the pope was too soft, too conciliatory, too quick to take the blame for offenses that were not one-sided. But those critics were the minority. Most praised the pope's actions and came to respect him as a great global leader. Because he saw the present situation on the ground for what it was and took action to change that situation, he was able to take steps toward realizing his vision. By being fully aware of what was going on in the moment, he was able to lead the Church confidently into the future.

Seeing Truth in the Moment

Being present in the moment is equally imperative for any leader. Far too often, CEOs have the same level of awareness as the emperor in the classic children's tale, "The Emperor's New Clothes." They walk around oblivious to the truth of the situation, choosing blindness to what is obvious, while assistants and associates who do see remain silent. These executives are inattentive to the people who are a part of their vision, and unaware of the problems on the ground.

Employees, of course, are partly responsible—the CEO holds the purse strings and it's difficult to criticize the person holding the purse strings—but ultimately the responsibility is the CEO's and the CEO's alone.

If you want to lead your company in the right direction, you have to help people understand that you want the truth, even when the truth is hard. You have to foster a corporate culture where honesty is rewarded. You have to train your eye to discern fact from fiction and learn how be attentive to every aspect of your company's business, from the hours the people you employ work to the quality of the product or service you offer. You have to do that because in business anything less is a recipe for disaster.

On the most basic level, it's a problem because a solid understanding of a company's strengths and weaknesses is required if you're going to steer the business in the right direction. If you're ill with the stomach flu, but only tell the doctor you have a headache, he's going to prescribe the wrong medicine, one that won't do anything to cure your real ailment and might in fact make it worse. The same goes for a company's fortunes. If you as an executive or CEO don't have an accurate understanding of what's going right and what's going wrong, you're likely to make decisions based on false premises that can, in the long run, do real damage to the company.

Likewise, realizing your vision for your company means you have to know if the things happening in your company right now, in the present moment, are moving you closer to that vision or farther away from it. Are your HR policies just? Are they helping build company loyalty? Do people in the company feel rewarded and satisfied? Is the corporate culture helping them move closer to God and live virtuous lives? What about the product? Is it superior? Is its price competitive? How do people in the market perceive it?

All those answers can only be ascertained by attentiveness to the present moment. Only when they're answered in the affirmative, can you successfully pursue your vision. That's why you have to watch, listen, and move quickly to take responsibility for whatever problems exist in the company or the public's perception of it. You can't pass the buck, and you can't do your best imitation of an ostrich, hiding your head in the sand and hoping problems will go away if you pretend not to see them. Like John Paul II, you have to hear that cricket chirping in the midst of a bustling city. That cricket, after all, may be the factor on which all your success hinges.

Know Where You're Going

Vision is where it starts. There's no getting around it. Whether you're a pope, a CEO, or an entrepreneur working out of his garage, you've got to have a vision. You need to know where you're going and why you're going there. You need goals—where you want to take the company or organization you're leading in five, ten, and twenty years. You need purpose—why you're doing what you're doing. Your vision is what helps you and all those working with you realize why your work matters. It keeps you focused on what's most important and clarifies your thoughts and actions.

That vision is exactly the type of vision John Paul II had.

As pope, he had a clear vision of his pontificate from the very start. In his first encyclical, *Redemptor Hominis*, he outlined the themes that would echo throughout his twenty-seven-year papacy: (1) Continue fully and faithfully implementing the ideals, goals, and reforms of the Second Vatican Council; (2) Promote a culture of life; and (3) Defend freedom while fighting oppression and materialism.

John Paul's vision was rooted in the problems all around him. He had seen in Poland what the denial of human freedom could do. He had also seen what the disregard for the sanctity of human life, which came into horrific focus in Poland under the Nazis, could do to a culture. He knew from his close, personal relationships with married couples how much help men and women needed understanding the vocation of marriage and the gift of their sexuality. He knew from his interactions with Catholics around the world, both lay and religious, that the hopes of Vatican II were going unrealized—or worse, its message perverted—in countless dioceses.

With a clear understanding of both the why and the what, John Paul II focused with laser-like precision on pursuing his vision. He never played it safe. He went to the limits again and again in order to do what was right. That wasn't easy, but his vision guided him through it all. It kept him faithful, and it kept him motivated. He knew what Christ was asking of him. He knew what the Church needed. He planned his days, weeks, months, and years to that end.

Because of that, he successfully led the Church into the twenty-first century, giving it a new way of articulating ancient truths about the Faith, the human person, freedom, dignity, sexuality, politics, and more. He traveled the world in order to teach people

1. Saying goodbye to John Paul II: My last audience (Courtesy of Arturo Mari)

2. Swearing-in on May 6, 1987
I swear I will faithfully, loyally and honorably serve the Supreme Pontiff John Paul II and his legitimate successors, and also dedicate myself to them with all my strength, sacrificing if necessary also my life to defend them. I assume this same commitment with regard to the Sacred College of Cardinals whenever the See is vacant.

Furthermore I promise to the Commanding Captain and my other superiors, respect, fidelity and obedience. This I swear! May God and our Holy Patrons assist me!
(Courtesy of Arturo Mari)

3. Our recruit school class with our sergeant (first left, back row) and the hand-to-hand combat instructor (center back row) (Courtesy of Stefan Meier)

4. In full armor (Courtesy of Stefan Meier)

5. With three of my friends in the Vatican gardens: (from the right) Roland Huwiler, Daniel Wicki, Hermann Baettig and I. (Courtesy of Stefan Meier)

2.

3.

4.   5.

6.

7.

8.

9.

6. In love in Rome: Michelle and I in front of St. Angel's Castle (Courtesy of Andreas Widmer)

7. With my grandfather on the day of my swearing-in (Courtesy of Arturo Mari)

8. John Paul II thanking my parents for my service on the day of my swearing-in (Courtesy of Arturo Mari)

9. On graduation day at Merrimack College with my friends, Father Arthur Johnson, OSA, and Fr. Peter Gori, OSA (Courtesy of Michelle Widmer)

10.

10. The Reagans arrive at the Vatican
for an official visit. I am the guard standing
at attention at the right.
(Courtesy of Arturo Mari)

11.

11. When Harry Belafonte visited
John Paul II, I asked him to sign my glove
for my mom. (Courtesy of Arturo Mari)

12. Holy Thursday Mass at St. Peter's
where I was one of the honor guard next to
the Pope. This was the longest time I ever
had to stand still. I think it was 4 hours.
(Courtesy of Arturo Mari)

**13. The group of guards during our last
meeting with John Paul II:** (from the
right) Patrick Gubler, Daniel Wicki,
Hubert Lingg, Thomas Broger and I
(Courtesy of Arturo Mari)

12.

13.

14.

15.

16.

17.

14. Standing still . . . Sentinel duty at the entrance to the pope's summer residence at Castel Gandolfo (Courtesy of Stefan Meier)

15. Gratitude. The pope always invited the group protecting him at his summer residence to his offices to thank them for their service. We brought along the two sisters who cooked for us during our time there. (Courtesy of Arturo Mari)

16. Service in civil clothes (Courtesy of Arturo Mari)

17. John Paul II greeted Poland's communist dictator, General Wojciech Jaruzelski, with as much kindness as he greeted its first democratically elected president, Lech Walesa. (Courtesy of Arturo Mari)

18. Returning in formation from the swearing-in ceremony (Courtesy of Arturo Mari)

19. Aligning the formation (Courtesy of Arturo Mari)

20.

21.

20. With my 4-year-old nephew Michael when he visited me in the Swiss Guards
(Courtesy of Stefan Meier)

21. With my nephew Michael 18 years later
(Courtesy of Michelle Widmer)

22. My nephew Matthias' swearing-in 24 years after my own
(Courtesy of Arturo Mari)

22.

23. Visiting John Paul II with Michelle and her parents (Courtesy of Arturo Mari)

24. Back in (temporary) service after 20 years (Courtesy of Andreas Widmer)

that vocabulary, making more trips than the all of his predecessors combined. He defended the Church's teachings at great personal risk. And in all that, he changed the lives of millions.

The Basics of a Successful Vision for Your Business
That same kind of planning goes into every successful business. If you want to lead your company someplace good, you've got to have a good vision. And what does that entail?

Let us first look at what that does *not* entail.

A good vision is not simply seeing a way toward short-term financial profit. The ultimate goal of any business can never be profit. The relationship between profit and business is like that of oxygen and life. You need oxygen to live, but the goal of life isn't the intake of oxygen. So too with business. Your business needs to make a profit in order to survive, but in and of itself, profit is not the ultimate goal. It's a means to an end. That end, that ultimate purpose, is determined by your vision.

The same goes for goals like "being rich" or "being powerful." Those aren't visionary. They're selfish goals based on selfish desires. They don't really get you anywhere. I should know.

For years I chased after riches. No matter how much money I made, I never felt it was enough. I always needed more. My thirst was never quenched. That's what happens to all who make money their ultimate goal. If that's all you're after, it will be never be enough. You will never feel satisfied. The hole won't be filled, not for you and not for those working with you toward that goal. The emptiness that comes from pursuing something as pedestrian as wealth will undermine, rather than strengthen, your company in the long run. It will lead to compromises, burn out, and a poorer quality good or service.

Similarly, "growth" and "success" don't qualify as vision. Both are too vague. Growth can mean many things and, depending on what stage your company is at, it's a fairly relative term. In strict percentages, growth for a start-up looks very different from growth for a multi-billion dollar corporation. Different types of growth are possible for the two, and they can't be held to the same system of measurement. Likewise, growth in numbers isn't all that matters. There are types of growth that can't be quantified—growth in abilities, personal maturity, understanding, and wisdom. Those, however, are as important or more than growth in market size and profit shares.

Profit, money, and simple growth can't define a leader's vision. So what does?

Like John Paul II's vision, a successful vision for a company or an organization needs to be centered on the human person. A business, after all, is a community of persons. It is made up of a group of individuals working together to serve other individuals. Whatever your vision is, it needs to take those persons into account. What do your customers, stakeholders, and employees need? Are you giving that to them? Is your work helping them live fuller, richer lives? Does it enhance or uphold human dignity? Those are the questions that keep your vision person-centered.

Likewise, your vision should capture the imagination of those who are part of it. It should inspire employees and stakeholders, much as John Paul's vision inspired an army of priests, religious, and laymen. Your vision needs to do this because a leader can't realize his vision alone. It always takes more than one man to actualize goals and dreams, and if a leader's vision doesn't inspire and excite others, it's not a vision that can endure.

Seven Fund, the organization I helped found, has an overarching vision of helping struggling third-world economies find solutions to poverty rooted in the principles of free enterprise. My partner and I, as well as those who work with us, share a firm commitment to the free market system and a common belief that that system is the way out for people trapped in poverty. That vision energizes us. It's what makes us excited to walk in the door every day and gives purpose to all the mundane tasks involved in any enterprise.

It's easy to see how an idea like fighting poverty can be inspiring. But bringing a great product to market—a product that helps people communicate better, allows for the faster delivery of information, or facilitates family life—can be just as exciting. We're physical creatures living in a material world, and what goes on in the material world, what we experience in our bodies, affects what goes on in our souls. You can't make goods that are truly good and services that truly serve without in some way enriching the human experience.[17] If you understand that and incorporate that understanding into your vision, your team will understand that as well. Your vision will become a source of inspiration.

A vision needs to be challenging and all employees in the company need to earnestly do their best to live up to it. General Electric has been motivating its employees for years with a vision of bringing "good things to life." Google says "do no evil." ServiceMasters says "to honor God in all we do." These are great visions, and challenging ones. And rightly so: A vision should call on people to push themselves to heights unknown and draw on wells of talent they didn't know they had. It should ask them to give something of themselves for the sake of others. The act of realizing the company or organization's vision helps people become more fully themselves. That's what will make work fulfilling. That's what will give life to the employees as well as the customer, clients, or demographics served.

***

For the first several days I served as a Swiss Guard, I remained within the confines of Vatican City. There, for as foreign as much of it was to me, was also a great deal of the familiar. The shopkeepers and postmasters worked hard to build friendships with the guards. I felt welcome. The Swiss Guard's barracks were almost like a mini-Switzerland, with geraniums in the courtyard and Swiss beer always on tap. To a young man like myself, one who had rarely before ventured outside of his small village, Vatican City felt not all that different. It was manageable, safe, almost familiar.

The city of Rome proper was an altogether different matter. Its fast-paced life crashed like violent waves on the Vatican's peaceful shores. On my first day out in the city, I almost drowned in those waves.

That day, as I prepared to explore the city, I was stopped in my tracks by the traffic at the border between Vatican City and Rome, the street right in front of the Swiss Guard barracks. I waited and waited for the pedestrian light, but even once it turned green, the traffic did not stop. Every time I put a foot onto the street, cars simply honked and swerved, but made no attempt to slow down. I continued trying for a few minutes, once even putting both feet onto the street, only to jump back onto the sidewalk to save my life. I was dumfounded. "What is this? This chaos is too much for me," I thought.

I was about to return to the safety of the barracks, when I heard a voice cry out, "Helvetice, why do you stand here so perplexed?"

The cry came from a relatively short man with a round red face, oversized glasses, and a shaven head. He was dressed in blue coveralls, reminiscent of auto mechanic garb. It was the pope's Latin teacher, Father Reggie Foster (which explained why he addressed me by the Latin word for Switzerland).

"Take courage!" the little priest shouted in a high-pitched voice. "Be one with this perfect chaos. Make it yours and it will obey you."

As he spoke, he began to slowly walk backwards into the busy intersection, his gaze locked with mine. He never flinched. There was a concert of honking, cars swerved around him screeching, and drivers swore at him from their open windows. But not one car so much as touched the man who stood in the middle of the intersection, wildly gesticulating with both arms, to underscore his message to me.

Father Reggie is almost worth a book in himself. He was a stubborn little man who insisted on wearing blue coveralls (purchased annually from the JCPenney in Milwaukee, Wisconsin) instead of clerics, and battled John Paul endlessly over whether the correct spelling of the pope's Latin name began with a "J" or an "I." (The pope won while he was alive, but it's *Ioannes*, not *Joannes* on his tombstone). Battles with the successor to St. Peter aside, Father Reggie's foray into the streets of Rome exemplifies what it means to bridge the paradox between a vision for the future and attentiveness to the present moment. He knew where he wanted to go—across the street—and he knew where that particular street happened to be—Rome. That meant he couldn't cross it like he would a street in Lucerne or Milwaukee. The circumstances of where he was required a calm, confident foray into chaos, which happens to be the only way to cross a busy intersection in the Eternal City. Father Reggie stayed focused on where he was going and where he was, so seemingly against all odds, he made it across the street.

Eventually, I did too.

Action Item: A Mission for Your Life

John Paul II had a mission for his life. What's your mission? Spend thirty minutes writing your own personal mission statement. Be specific. Cover all the pertinent areas of your life and roles you play. Next, write down your short and long-term goals for each: family, work, friends, your social environment, and your personal development. Finally, come up with an action plan, writing out the actions in both the present moment and the years ahead that will help you turn the goal and vision into a reality.

Review this mission statement and action plan at least once a year, revising as appropriate.

Questions for Reflection

1. Describe the vision or mission of your company. How does it compare to the criteria for a successful vision outlined in this chapter? Is it human-centered? Inspiring? Challenging? Is it lived out? Do you live according to the vision of your own company? If not, what about it needs to change? List five changes that you can implement in your own behavior to reflect your company's vision in what you do every day and how you do it.

2. Describe a time where you or your manager pursued only short-term financial profit and not the true vision of the company. What were the consequences of that, both in the short-term and long-term?

3. How honest is your team when it comes to telling you the truth about any given situation? Do you encourage honesty and forthrightness? How can you be more honest? How can you invite more honesty from others? List five concrete actions.

4. What do you need to change about yourself so that you're more attentive to the moment? Name at least three concrete things you can do daily.

Chapter Six

Know Your Team:
The Value of Cultivating
and Synchronizing Talent

"To one he gave five talents; to another, two; to a third, one—to each according to his ability. Then he went away."

Matthew 25:15

[T]he person who works desires not only due remuneration for his work; he also wishes that within the production process, provision be made for him to be able to know that in his work, even on something that is owned in common, he is working "for himself." This awareness is extinguished within him in a system of excessive bureaucratic centralization, which makes the worker feel that he is just a cog in a huge machine moved from above, that he is for more reasons than one a mere production instrument rather than a true subject of work with an initiative of his own.

—Blessed John Paul II

On the morning of May 6, 1987, I awakened in the barracks at 5:30 a.m. to the sound of drumming. After a quick breakfast, I put on my gala uniform and headed to the courtyard for morning call. Gathered there were the thirty-three of us who had entered during the previous twelve months, plus about twenty of the older guards. Because we kept watch at the papal palace round the clock, this was the largest possible assembly of the guards, not just for the day, but also for the year.

After entering formation and answering roll call, we marched to the *Aula Della Benedizione* (Benediction Hall). That's the hall directly behind St. Peter's Square, the one whose central window opens up to the famous balcony where the new pope appears immediately following his election.

Epigraph. Encyclical Letter on Human Work *Laborem Exercens* (September 14, 1981), 15.

We entered the hall in lockstep, led by our commanding officers, the Swiss Guard flag, and four drummers. It was an imposing sight, and as we marched in full formation to our seats, I caught a glimpse of my grandfather, standing to the side, saluting me with tears in his eyes.

Besides my grandfather, my parents and other relatives were also present in the hall, as were the families and pastors of most of the new guards. They had traveled down from Switzerland for this annual celebration that both commemorated the swearing in of the new guards and paid tribute to our fallen comrades.

After we took our seats, the pope entered, blessing the families and the new guards as he moved toward the altar. There, along with many of our parish priests, he offered Mass. Once Mass was over, he changed out of his vestments and prayed quietly for a few minutes. Then he invited the new recruits to introduce him to our parents. In the Swiss Guards the order of sequence usually goes by height and not by name, so I (at 6'9") was one of the first called up.

In the days leading up to the audience, I'd given a great deal of thought to what I would say and how I could introduce my parents. But as we approached, all the carefully rehearsed words failed me. I was emotional and couldn't speak. Fortunately, the Holy Father took the initiative and spoke for me.

"Ah, Andreas, my tallest guard!" he said, reaching out his hands, one to my mother and one to my father as I stood between them.

"You can be proud of your son," he continued.

My father managed to say something about how happy he was to have his son serving the successor of St. Peter, and John Paul nodded with understanding. He then turned to my mother, took both her hands, looked into her tear-filled eyes, and said, "Thank you for giving me my tallest guard." He then put his hand on her forehead and blessed her.

As we stood there, I realized that each of my parents had grabbed my hand. It was the first time that I felt they were holding onto me instead of me holding onto them.

That day, something changed between my parents and me. When they looked at me, they no longer saw a child, but a man who was part of John Paul II's world. Something changed in me as well. I understood for the first time that I was part of something much bigger than myself or even the Swiss Guards. I saw myself as John Paul II's co-worker, as a collaborator in his vision for man, the Church, and the world. I knew my role was a small one, but that day I realized just how important even small roles in great missions can be. When I left that audience hall, it was with renewed enthusiasm for my work and a deepened appreciation for the opportunity I'd been given.

That was no coincidence.

During the twenty-seven years of his pontificate, John Paul II was one of the most famous and recognizable men on the planet. His life inspired hundreds of millions of people, and his words shaped the history of the latter half of the twentieth century. The Holy Spirit had a lot to do with that. So did the team of people who worked alongside the pope, planning his trips, delivering his messages, and making the engines of the Vatican machinery run smoothly.

It took more than one man to further John Paul's vision, and he knew that. He understood that great leaders need great teams. He also understood that great leaders make great teams, that it is the leader's responsibility to cultivate the virtues and habits necessary for success in those working with him and to help them understand the importance of what they do. Accordingly, he took great care in assembling, leading, and motivating his team.

At that, he excelled.

Assembling a Team

At the outset of his pontificate, like any other CEO, John Paul II needed to assemble an executive team. He needed to select the men who would be responsible, at the highest levels, for helping him implement his vision. He could have done this immediately, making sweeping changes as soon as he was elected. But he didn't. He made some key appointments early, but for the most part, he waited until he felt the right time and right person had come along. He observed the nature of the Vatican, the nature of those around him, and only slowly, after careful deliberation, made changes to the staff and structure he inherited from John Paul I and Paul VI.

Whenever a position opened, he filled it with someone who shared his vision; someone who also was capable, secure, and independent. He gave people freedom to realize his vision in their own way.

The pope didn't assemble his leadership team out of men who were virtual clones of himself. Rather, he brought together individuals with starkly different personalities and backgrounds. There was the shrewd and political Cardinal Augustino Casaroli, who as Secretary of State finessed both diplomats and dictators with great skill. Then there was the shy and reflective Cardinal Joseph Ratzinger, whose methodical mind brought clarity to the Congregation for the Doctrine of the Faith, the office responsible for the teaching of Catholic doctrine. Smiling Cardinal Francis Arinze of Nigeria, appointed as prefect of the Congregation for Divine Worship, had a gentle and friendly demeanor that made him a naturally disarming defender of the Catholic Liturgy.

There were others, each different, but all sharing John Paul's vision and uniquely suited to the tasks required of them. That was what mattered to the pope—that they could do their job and do it well. This lead to a shift in the corporate culture: Where Italians had previously dominated the Vatican hierarchy, holding ten or more of the top positions, under John Paul II they claimed but four. Power and influence also mattered little to John Paul, who changed the makeup of the College of Cardinals to more closely reflect the make-up of the world's Catholic population. By the time of his death, 40 percent of voting cardinals came from developing countries. When he first took office, the percentage was less than ten.

During the years I served in the Vatican, I saw several men I'd gotten to know personally elevated to positions of power. Unfailingly, those men were among the priests and bishops who had impressed me the most. I can't ever remember thinking, "What? Him? What's the pope thinking?" The selections were always wise, the result of John Paul II's careful attention to individuals, keen sense of personality, and careful reflection on the choice before him.

Later, once those team members were in place, John Paul built on their strengths. None of his top cardinals were perfect. The pope knew that as well as anyone else. But he chose to help them focus on and develop their strengths, rather than lament their weaknesses. In certain situations, he would send personal envoys who had an ability that made them uniquely suited for a specific task—handling a difficult negotiation or intervening in a sensitive situation—but then turn the long-term work on the issue over to others. For example, rather than send one of the Vatican's top diplomats (who are all priests, bishops, or cardinals) to represent the Church at the Beijing Conference on Women, he instead asked the most qualified person—American laywoman, law professor, and international human rights scholar Mary Ann Glendon.

Priests and bishops can get as territorial as anyone else when it comes to departments and jobs. It's not that there were never turf wars under John Paul II's watch or that no eyebrows were ever raised when he made a staffing change. But the pope tried to minimize squabbles as much as possible, and when it mattered most, he didn't allow those types of concerns to prevent him from matching the right person with the right task. In his eyes, what was at stake was too important to submit to Vatican politics.

The Mark of a True Leader

In that, John Paul understood what so many CEOs don't. One of the marks of great leadership is the ability to match the right person with the right task. You must be a synchronizer of talent, understanding what's really required for each and every job and knowing what skills are necessary to accomplish specific tasks.

This is not to say that the task is more important than the person who achieves it. Quite the contrary. But many executives mistakenly try to force a person to conform to a position like a small child tries to force a square block into a circular hole. Doing so is counterproductive, both with respect to achieving the goal and to the person in question.

My most painful mistakes in business resulted from me doing exactly that. I failed to think of my employees and goals honestly and give due consideration to who would be best at what task or who could develop in a certain direction. I didn't do my homework or take the time to really talk with them about their careers, training, goals, and need for guidance and improvement.

Unlike John Paul II, I wasn't attentive enough to the true nature of my employees, and even when I did have a suspicion that a certain person wasn't the best choice for a certain task, I did my best to avoid admitting that. I was more focused on the short-term needs of the company, not on what would be best for both the company and the individual in the long-term.

The way to avoid these mistakes is simply to take more time with personnel decisions. As a manager, you must meet with all your direct employees regularly, engaging them in conversation about their goals, talents, and past experiences. You also have to give serious thought to what they need to grow professionally and, importantly, be honest with them when something isn't working out.

I know a great many executives who shrink from these kinds of conversations. But they don't have to be unpleasant. They can actually be both enjoyable and constructive. But that depends on you and your ability to lead and encourage your team with the attitude of a coach.

Leading as a Coach

When it comes to leadership, there are critics and there are coaches. The critic's primary objective is not the person but the project. In the critic's eyes, the person is a means to an end. The coach, on the other hand, is someone who keeps the whole person in mind, with a special focus on the employee's potential and the progress they're making toward achieving that potential. A coach's feedback may be tough, but it's also hopeful and expectant. He cares about the goal, but he knows that the person always matters more.

John Paul II was a coach. Whether he was meeting with top aides or lowly guards like myself, he never compromised the truth. He was realistic about problems, obstacles, and the like. As gentle as he was, there was no sugar coating of hard facts. But he approached those problems with a "can-do" attitude. He had every expectation that obstacles could be overcome, and he always let you know he was on your side.

I'll never forget what he said to me once I made the decision to leave the Swiss Guards:

"Go out into the world and bring what you have learned here with you: I have great hopes for you."

John Paul II made it clear that he believed in me. He, in fact, believed in all people—in the power and potential for good we all possess as creatures made in the image of God. He had seen the worst mankind could do—Nazi death camps, Stalinist purges, the repression of basic rights and freedoms—and he still had confidence in man. He wanted man to have confidence in man too. That was the point of pep talks such as the ones he gave me and the other guards. He understood the basic yearnings in all of us—the yearning for meaning, for greatness, for being valued, trusted, loved, and accepted—and he knew how to speak to those yearnings. He pointed us toward the One who could fulfill them— God—and made us feel that such heights of glory weren't beyond our reach.

John Paul II also knew how to make the most menial tasks of guard duty feel as important as the grandest acts of political diplomacy and apostolic ministry. He urged us to see why our work mattered, why we mattered, and he inspired us to give our all to everything we undertook.

He did that, not just by giving benevolent guidance, but also by building a personal rapport with us. He took the time to talk to all who served in the Vatican. He paid attention to people, and through the simplest acts of recognition, helped everyone working with him see that they weren't anonymous cogs working in a giant bureaucratic machine, but rather important contributors to the most important work in the world. That same personal rapport is what made it possible for his advisors to both give and receive honest counsel. His team trusted him because they knew him.

With the Swiss Guards specifically, one of the ways he did this was to share a dinner with us during the summer when we were at Castel Gandolfo and his schedule was not as busy. The guards would prepare a Swiss meal and then spend the evening entertaining the pope with music, singing, or a slide presentation about our life as guards. The pope visibly enjoyed himself during these evenings, laughing at the guards' jokes and asking questions about our work. He really wanted to know what this or that job was like and how certain tasks were performed. Through his questions, the guards felt both cared-for and affirmed.

John Paul also took the time, whenever he could, to baptize the children born to the Swiss Guards. His secretary would call immediately after the birth and ask how the mother and child were doing, then tell the parents that the Holy Father would be happy to baptize the child if they wished—which, of course, most did.

The Corporate Coach
If the leader of a billion Catholics can take the time to build a rapport with his employees, there is no CEO or manager who can't

do the same. Personal knowledge and personal contact shape the spirit of a team. The better you know your employees and the more comfortable they feel with you, the more you can lead them as a coach and not a critic. That's yet another reason why perks such as separate elevators and entrances for the CEO or senior partners are such a bad idea. They feed the "us versus them" mentality that plagues so many firms. They also make it very difficult for a CEO to ever put a person before a goal. After all, if you never see the person, how is he going to matter more to you than the goal at the forefront of your mind?

So how do you build that rapport? Depending on the size of your department or business there are lots of ways, from company Christmas parties and picnics to a monthly breakfast. Regular meetings and evaluations are important. In those meetings you should listen as well as talk, striving to discover how the person sees his job, his role in the company, and what he thinks he needs to do his job better. Simply asking questions from time to time as John Paul did is also important: Where are you from? Do you have a family? What do you love doing? Little answers to little questions go a long way toward helping you form a picture of the person in front of you, and letting him know that you see him as more than just a job title.

When you lead as a coach, you put person-centered ethics into practice and help your employees fulfill their God-given potential. Not coincidentally, you also make them better employees, more capable of and more willing to work hard at building a stronger company. That's something that makes both good human sense and good business sense.

***

Once you've built your team and fostered their growth, what can you expect from them? You can expect someone like Archbishop Henri Lemaitre.

I met the archbishop one evening in 1987 while I was standing guard in the San Damaso courtyard. He was passing by on his way to a meeting, and, mostly out of boredom, I struck up a conversation with the man. He appeared fairly non-descript at first, older and wearing the typical Roman collar. His passport told me that he was the archbishop who ran the Vatican Embassy in Denmark and represented the Vatican there, as well as in Sweden, Norway, Finland, and Iceland. After a short conversation, we discovered that he knew my father. Something told me this man had stories to tell, so I asked him if we could continue our conversation over dinner the next night. He agreed, and when we did continue that conversation I discovered my instincts were right.

As it turns out, this man was the Vatican's version of 007. Over the years he served the pope in Vietnam and Cambodia, where he was nearly executed by an angry mob; as well as in Uganda, where he was tasked with negotiating with the country's ruthless dictator, Idi Amin. The archbishop had supported underground churches in countries where the Faith was banned or where government-controlled puppet churches operated. He'd also worked to prevent the execution of priests and directed money for missions to their rightful recipients. He did the sort of things that one only reads about in books or sees in movies, and he did them with almost no outside help.

Where the Vatican sent Lemaitre, communication was often difficult, if not impossible. In the midst of revolutions and riots, there was no way for him to check with the Vatican about what moves he should make or risks he should take. He made those calls for himself, transitioning seamlessly from follower to leader when all channels of communication went silent. He had the ability to carry out the pope's wishes even when he hadn't been specifically told what those wishes were. He was able to do that because he possessed the diplomatic skills the job required, as well as courage, passion, and an understanding of the pope's vision.

That's the type of team member John Paul II's leadership style cultivated. That's the kind of team member every business, big or small, needs.

Synchronizing Talent

How well do the right persons and the right tasks match up in your company?

This simple exercise can help you find the answer to that question.

Step 1:   Make a list of the key positions in your company or group. Describe in clear terms what each job needs in terms of human talent and ability. Feel free to distinguish between essentials and "nice to haves."

Step 2:   Think of your key employees (direct reports) and make a list of their key strengths and talents. Also note what your long-term vision would be for each one. Who is that individual at his best? What could each person achieve if he stretched?

Step 3:   Explore how well the two lists overlap. Is the right person in the right job? If so, what training or mentoring could bring him to the next level? If not, what job would be better for him? Can you help him get there?

Questions for Reflection

1. Who was the best manager you ever had? Describe what made this leader great. Did this person lead as a coach or a critic? How did he or she bring out the best in you as an employee?

2. Who was the worst manager you ever had. Describe what made this person difficult to work for. How did this manager's leadership style affect your work and the work of your fellow employees?

3. Describe the type of manager you want to be. How close is reality matching up to that vision? What, if anything, needs to change? How do you think those changes will affect your team?

Chapter Seven

Live as a Witness:
The Testimony of Right Action

"Amen, I say to you, whatever you did for one of these least brothers of mine, you did for me."

Matthew 25:40

The relationship between man's freedom and God's law, which has its intimate and living centre in the moral conscience, is manifested and realized in human acts. It is precisely through his acts that man attains perfection as man, as one who is called to seek his Creator of his own accord and freely to arrive at full and blessed perfection by cleaving to him.

—Blessed John Paul II

I n Rome, the gypsies are everywhere—the subways, the streets, the churches. Some are thieves and pickpockets. Some are street performers. Most are beggars. They have made an art of it.

Visitors to Rome often find the gypsy beggars annoying. They're never sure whether to give them money or not. The Catholic pilgrims are especially torn. One of the first things most are told by knowledgeable Romans is never give anything to a gypsy, that they're all con artists and thieves. But then they see a sad-eyed woman with an even sadder-eyed child, and callously walking past her feels like the last thing any Christian should do.

The Romans, however, don't have such qualms. They hate the gypsies, and have made as much of an art out of hating them, as the gypsies have made out of begging.

Because Romans primarily staff the Vatican, running all the businesses inside Vatican City and holding a large chunk of the

---

Epigraph. Encyclical Letter on the Church's Moral Teaching *Veritatis Splendor* (August 6, 1993), 71.

ecclesial posts, you can guess what the prevailing attitude toward the gypsies is there. But during the time I lived in Vatican City, that animosity began to wane because of John Paul II.

John Paul II knew how the gypsies were perceived inside the Vatican's walls, and he disliked that about as much as he disliked the fact that homeless men, women, and children slept on the Vatican's doorstep. So, in May of 1987, about six months after I arrived in Rome, he agreed to Mother Teresa's request to open a seventy-four-bed shelter inside the Vatican. It opened the following winter.

As soon as the sisters began taking in guests, the Swiss Guards began volunteering there. Our job was to watch out for trouble-makers and keep the sisters safe. While we did that, we helped the sisters out with the various tasks involved in running such an enterprise. I usually took on the job of helping them serve dinner, and was unfailingly impressed by the sisters' simplicity, humility, and love. I also was impressed by the actions of the pope.

Not only did John Paul II make the unprecedented move of opening the shelter inside the Papal Palace, but, also unprece-dented and perhaps more surprising, he held audiences for the gypsies and homeless of Rome. In the midst of traveling the world, meeting with prime ministers, and shaping the way the Faith was taught and lived, he regularly took time to be with those who most Romans considered the dregs of their city. The significance of that was never lost on the gypsies who came to the audiences. As I stood guard, I would watch their faces. They were different in that room than they were on the outside. They were, in a way, more themselves. They lost the anonymous look of the beggar and reflected instead their God-given dignity as individuals.

In meeting with the Holy Father, those gypsies and beggars remembered who they were. And so did we. After those audi-ences, none of us in Vatican City could look at gypsies in quite the same way. John Paul II's actions affected us all. They helped us see the truth of the situation, and they helped each of us act with greater virtue.

That's the power leaders possess. By their actions, they shape the beliefs and actions of those serving under them. That's why it's so important that a leader's actions be the right ones. In all his actions, great and small, he must live as a witness to truth. He must never forget what our mothers so insistently told us: Actions speak louder than words.

Why Actions Matter

Actions matter because all actions (and inaction) have consequences. Some consequences may be small. Some may be earth shattering. Regardless, everything we do, every action we take, in some way affects ourselves, our environment, or the lives of others.

Consider, for example, how our actions affect us. If I want to become a piano player, the way to do that is not to sit around and think about becoming a piano player or spend my evenings poring over sheet music. The way to become a piano player is to practice the piano. If I perform the action of piano playing often enough, my actions will eventually make me that which I seek to become.

The same holds true for all our other actions. If I cheat at cards, I become a cheater. If I lie to my business partners, I become a liar. If I sleep around on my wife, I become an adulterer. Conversely, if I give to those in need, I become generous. If I hold my tongue when someone insults me, I become meek. If I control my anger and strength, I become gentle.

However, nothing I do can ever destroy my God-given dignity. But some actions will undermine that dignity and some actions will enhance it. For good or for ill, our actions define and shape us.

None of us live in a vacuum. Our actions don't only affect us. They also affect others for days, centuries, or millennia to come. After all, it was the sin of our first parents, Adam and Eve that led to original sin. They messed up, and the fruits of that were passed down to their children and every other human being who has since walked the face of this earth. Their actions had consequences that will last long past the day the sun stops shining.

My actions can do the same, even if not quite on such a grand scale. A kind word or a harsh word to my son today can shape his understanding of me, himself, and men in general, even God, for the rest of his life. How you treat a co-worker—such as lending a hand when a major deadline looms or not helping—can make the difference between them keeping their job or losing it. Both our good works and our bad works live on. Through the effect they have on others, they travel into history.

When you're a leader, those effects are amplified even more. Perform enough of those right or wrong actions, and it's not just yourself or one other person you affect, but the entire culture of your environment. Your temper can make your home a terrible place to be, where no one says what they think and where your children learn to respond to frustration with yelling and violence. The same applies to our work. My willingness to make questionable business deals will create a culture of dishonesty within the company. Mistakes will be covered up, numbers manufactured, and office supplies (or worse) filched.

What it comes down to is that if you want to create a happy, peaceful home, you have to act happily and peacefully. If you want an honest, hardworking team, you have to act honestly and diligently. You have to use your mind and your will to be aware of your actions and their consequences, and then undertake the actions that will produce the consequences you're after. No one (or almost no one) will do as you say. They will do as you do—so what you're doing had better be right.[18]

The Heart of Papal Action

In Chapter Three, I talked about the importance of ethics in helping us act rightly. They give us, I contended, a framework for choosing the good. Here I'll add that ethics, more than anything else, are shaped by the intellect. They're the product of clear moral reasoning.

We need clear moral reasoning. It gives shape or form to right actions. It doesn't, however, animate them. It doesn't give our actions the life and warmth they need in order to make us authentic and effective witnesses. In other words, ethics are the guide for right action, but they're not the heart of right action. John Paul II's person-centered ethics as a mere philosophical concept isn't what made us sit up and take notice when he held the hands of gypsy women or kissed babies with AIDS. His ethical framework isn't why countless young men and women followed him into the priesthood or religious life or why millions started living their faith more seriously. It's certainly not why I started living my faith more seriously.

There was something else there, something that gave life to all John Paul II did. More specifically, I think there were three attitudes that are essential to being a witness to truth and a leader through action: Knowledge, respect for human dignity, and love.

Knowledge

Let's start with knowledge. By knowledge, I don't necessarily mean book learning. Don't get me wrong. John Paul II was an admirably learned man. He had two doctorates, was an accomplished philosopher, author, and poet, and spoke at least eight languages fluently. He spent hours every day reading, writing, and studying. His knowledge of ideas, history, and culture enabled him to make informed choices and act rightly in any number of situations.

But John Paul learned through doing and listening as much as, if not more than, through reading. As a boy he played soccer with his Jewish neighbors. As a young man he worked in stone quarries and chemical plants. As a priest and bishop he spent long weekends hiking with married couples and young people. Once he became pope, he insisted on traveling the world, going to see his flock where they lived and worked, struggled and prayed. John

Paul II was always out there in the world, experiencing life and paying careful attention to all that happened around him. He was a student of life, and knew he had as much to learn from others as they did from him. He once wrote:

> Whenever I meet young people in my travels throughout the world, I wait first of all to hear what they want to tell me about themselves, about their society, about their Church. And I always point out: What I am going to say to you is not as important as what you are going to say to me. You will not necessarily say it to me in words; you will say it to me by your presence, by your song, perhaps by your dancing, by your skits, and finally, by your enthusiasm.[19]

John Paul II knew that if he wanted his actions to mean something to people, he had to know those people. He had to know the world as it was. He had to learn from the world so that it might learn from him.

A Respect for Human Dignity
In his observations of others, however, John Paul II never looked at people in general. He looked at people in particular. He saw faces and stories and all that goes into making each human person unique. He also saw Christ in every person. He saw the mark of God, who made man in his image, became man in order to save him, and destined man for an eternity with him. What John Paul II saw was each person's innate human dignity.

So he acted accordingly.

The pope strove to listen to others, to seek out their story and look them in they eye as they told it. He chose to take time during a busy day to ask the sisters cleaning his apartment about their ailing parents or wayward nieces. He chose to stop when passing through a large crowd in order to bless small children or talk to the wounded and the lame. No person was ever too insignificant to receive his notice because to him every person was a holy creation, made by the hand of God to hold the life of God within.

That attitude shaped the little details of his life—such as getting to know men like me who silently stood guard around him. It shaped the overarching goals of his papacy—such as helping men and women understand the true beauty and gift of human sexuality. It was always there, always evident, always palpable. You felt more important in John Paul II's presence than you did anywhere else. That wasn't because he was so important. You weren't basking in the glow of his papal majesty. It was because he saw how important you were and treated you that way. He saw dignity where no one else did. And so people like me, like those Roman gypsies, even like half-mad third world dictators, responded to what he did and said as we responded to no other. What he said and did mattered to us because we knew we mattered to him.

Love

"So faith, hope, love remain, these three; but the greatest one of these is love" (I Corinthians 13:13). Above all, love was the driving force behind all John Paul II's actions. By love, however, I don't mean what most people think love means. In today's culture, we tend to either oversexualize the term, or we use it as a synonym for "like." John Paul II, however, understood love in the classical sense, what Aristotle defined as "wanting for someone what one thinks good, for his sake and not for one's own, and being inclined, so far as one can, to do such things for him."[20]

In other words, as John Paul II explained in his book *Love and Responsibility*, love doesn't begin with infatuation. Love actually begins when infatuation ends. It is a choice, an action where I do something purely for the good of the other, regardless of my own interests and objectives. The measure of love, he continued, is the degree to which I pursue their good through my actions.[21]

When understood in that light, love becomes something that can give form to the human community, that can unite people in a common desire to seek one another's good. Love, or the lack of it, shapes the world. Love makes us responsible for the condition of the world: The shape it takes is the shape we give it. It is the product of how well or how poorly we've accepted Christ's command to love God with our whole heart, mind, and strength and to love others as ourselves.

St. John of the Cross, a Spanish mystic to whom John Paul had a great devotion, wrote that, "at the end of your life, you will be judged by your love."

Reflecting on that statement, the pope commented that if we truly believe what St. John writes, then our task each day is to make the commandment to love the center of our life. It has to guide and inspire everything we do.

That is exactly what love did for him. John Paul II's life wasn't about him. Instead, his life was about loving God and loving others. John Paul II gave up everything to do that—his acting, his professorship, his freedom, his privacy, his health. He sacrificed all his own desires for the good of a billion plus individuals. Those who interacted with him in almost any way perceived that. We saw love in his eyes when he spoke to us. We read it in every encyclical he wrote and heard it in every speech he gave. His love was always there, giving life to every word and action. Because he loved, he always told the truth. Because he loved, he wanted all to know Christ. Because he loved, millions wanted to know Christ too.

Leading as a Witness

John Paul II understood the importance of his actions. Those actions themselves were animated by his intimate knowledge of the human person, his respect for human dignity, and by his conscious choice to desire and pursue the good of others before his own good, in short, by his love. That's much of what made the pope such an effective leader. If we translate those principles into practice, that's what can help make us effective leaders as well.

How do we do that?

Leading by Example

Leading by example starts with you and how you conduct your own life. Are you honest, thrifty, responsible, and hardworking? Do you hold yourself to the same standards to which you hold your employees? Do you give yourself privileges and perks that you don't give to others? Do you stay away from questionable business practices and shady deals? If a greasy proposition does come your way, how do you respond? Do you dodge it or delegate it? Cave in or say no? Do you choose to do things that you would never ask someone you respect, like the pope or your grandmother, to do?

The answers to those questions matter. Your employees will follow your lead, and this in turn creates the company culture. As the CEO or owner, you are the personification of the company. Your answers to all those questions and more determine the moral direction your company takes.

It's also important to understand that the wrong answers to life's hard questions aren't mitigated because they were made with good intentions. That's consequentialism—allowing the end to justify the means—and in one way or another, consequentialism will lead you into trouble. The surest path is always the one paved by right actions. You are far more likely to be successful, at least in the long run, if you put principle above profit.

Besides, if the only way for your company to survive is by cheating or making questionable deals, then it's probably better just to let it die. A business is not a person. It's okay to abandon one, especially if doing so is the only way to uphold truth and human dignity.

Loving Your Employees

Your ability to lead by example also hinges on the extent to which you show your love for your employees. I know the idea of loving one's employees, of seeing them as friends and not just human resources, can sound a little strange at first. But loving your employees is what's required if you want to live and lead as a witness.

What is meant by "loving your employees"?

Consider your business as a group of friends, not a firm. Firms aren't moral agents. Firms don't have souls. The more you see the people who work for your business as individuals with moral responsibilities and a divinely ordained end, the less likely you are to start abdicating ethical obligations.

Loving your employees also requires remembering what real love is. John Paul II liked to quote Aristotle on this one, but for simplicity's sake, I like to quote the Italians. The Italians don't generally say, "I love you." Instead they say, *ti voglio bene*, literally "I want goodness for you," or "I want your good." That's an excellent summation of what love is: desiring the good of another and helping them realize that good.

When you understand love in that light, it becomes possible to see yourself as a "steward" of your employees' careers, of their professional fulfillment. God has entrusted to you the stewardship over this particular part of a person's life. Your goal should be to help that person become excellent at what they do. This is a form of love. By managing them well and wisely—giving them constructive feedback, assigning them responsibilities that allow them to use their God-given talents, and challenging them to grow in their abilities and knowledge—you help them find fulfillment and become, at least in one area, the person God made them to be.

You need to know your employees in order to do this. You can't swoop in at performance review time and be the voice on high dictating to them what's best. You have to seek to understand who they are, what strengths and weaknesses they possess, and what motivates them.

That's not always easy to do. Nor is it easy to separate your interests and the company's interests from each employee's individual interests. Yet when you have a holistic view of your employees, you see them not just as "money makers," but as human persons made up of minds, bodies, and souls, and having needs that transcend your own. This perspective makes it far easier to act toward them in such a way that their dignity is never compromised. The company will be stronger for that, and you will be a better leader.

Loving Your Foes, As Well As Your Friends
In Matthew's Gospel, Jesus made it clear that we can't just act rightly toward people we like. We also need to deal honestly and justly with those we don't like:

> "But I say to you, Love your enemies and pray for those who persecute you...For if you love those who love you, what reward have you? Do not even the tax collectors do the same? And if you salute only your brethren, what more are you doing than others? Do not even the Gentiles do the same?" Matthew 5:44, 46–47 RSV

The real test of leadership by example comes when you have to deal with competitors or with employees and colleagues who drive you a little (or very) crazy. Your ability to deal justly with those people says more about you and teaches others more about how they are expected to act than almost anything else you do.

As with so many other aspects of leadership, John Paul II was a master of dealing with those who were, at least to start with, less than fond of him and the Church.

During the years I served in the Swiss Guards, we greeted plenty of people who you wouldn't want to invite over to your house for dinner. One of those was the Dictator of Zaire, Mobutu Sese Seko. When he came to the Vatican in March of 1987, some of the guards were not pleased. Seko was a legendarily ruthless ruler, and it was difficult to understand why John Paul II would dignify the man with an audience. One of the older officers, however, put the discussion to rest.

First, he pointed out, we were soldiers and not judges. He explained that even a dictator represents his people and that receiving a head of state was first and foremost a nod to the nation. He asked whether any of us knew what the pope would say in the meeting. We did not. He then asked us what we would say. On that, we did have some strong opinions.

"Well," he concluded, "you can assume that the pope is going to say some of those very same things. But he can't say them if he doesn't receive him."

Point taken.

The same holds true with your company. If you don't speak with difficult employees or competitors, you can't build better relationships, find common ground, or learn to get along. If you don't treat them with knowledge, respect, and love, speaking with them is not going to do either them or you much good. You have to engage justly in order to get anywhere in your company and in the market. Good relationships matter. Good reputations matter. If you conduct your affairs with other companies according to right principles, even those companies considered shady or difficult, you positively affect the culture of corporate America as a whole.

***

Right actions animated by knowledge, respect, and love have the power to not only make your business more successful, but to help you and your employees become the people God made you to be. They shape you and define you, just as they shape and define the culture of your company. They do the heavy lifting that no HR department or employee handbook can do. Words and policies are meaningless unless they're incarnated in action.

John Paul knew that and lived that. That's why he met personally with the gypsies of Rome. More than any papal letter he could have penned, even more than the homeless shelter he asked Mother Teresa to open, the personal witness of him meeting with the gypsies, looking at them and embracing them changed the way the people of Vatican City and Rome saw the gypsies. He gave those of us who watched him an embodied reminder of their innate human dignity. He modeled for us the way we were supposed to treat them and everyone else on this planet.

He did that just as powerfully in his personal interactions with his staff, with the people he met as he traveled the world, and with some of the Church's and humanity's greatest enemies. He taught us through his knowledgeable, respectful, and loving actions how we should treat others. Because it was a lesson we saw lived and not just preached, it was a lesson we learned to live as well.

A Prayer for Help in Right Action

Breathe in me, O Holy Spirit, that my thoughts may all
   be holy.
Act in me, O Holy Spirit, that my work too, may be holy.
Draw my heart, O Holy Spirit, that I love but what is holy.
Strengthen me, O Holy Spirit, to defend all that is holy.
Guard me, then, O Holy Spirit, that I always may be holy.
Amen.

—St. Augustine

Questions for Reflection

1. Describe a situation where an action someone else took had a lasting consequence for you. What was the consequence? How was it good? How was it bad? Had that person acted differently, how would the consequences have been different?

2. Knowledge, respect, and love motivated John Paul II's actions. What other attitudes, good and bad, can motivate a person's actions? Think of your own actions over the past few days. What are some of the attitudes that have motivated those actions? By what do you want to be motivated? Write them on a paper card and put it where you can see it during the day.

3. How do you typically think of your employees or team? How well do you know them? What motivates your interactions with them? To put it another way: what makes you happy in their regard? What is a good next step for each of your employees in their professional development? What three steps can you take at the office to better pursue that good?

Chapter Eight

Live a Balanced Life:
All Things in Moderation

There is an appointed time for everything, and a time for every affair under the heavens.

Ecclesiastes 3:1

All men and women are entrusted with the task of crafting their own life: in a certain sense, they are to make of it a work of art, a masterpiece.

—Blessed John Paul II

Whenever I hear speculation in the newspaper that Cardinal so-and-so is vying for the throne of Peter, I shake my head and laugh. No cardinal wants to be pope. They know too well what goes into it, what the office demands. The work is endless, the responsibilities bone-crushing. There's no end to it, save death.

There's also the loneliness that can come with being pope. When you're elected to the papacy, you have to leave your old life behind. You give up everything, even your name. The new name you take when you ascend to the Chair of Peter symbolizes the new identity you're assuming. The old you is gone. The new you lives according to the demands of the Church and the expectations of Vatican protocol.

John Paul II, however, didn't completely buy into that line of thinking. When he could, he fought it. He didn't want to stop

Epigraph. Letter to Artists (April 4, 1999), 2.

enjoying life because he was now the pope. He didn't want to cut off ties to so much of what he loved. So, in the midst of Vatican demands and expectations, he carved out a space for himself in which he could find the peace, recreation, and laughter that he knew were essential to a well-ordered life.

Sports occupied a large chunk of that space.

Throughout his life, John Paul II was an avid sportsman. He loved skiing, hiking, canoeing, swimming—anything that kept him outdoors. As a priest, professor, and even bishop, he took his students and friends on long camping trips. That was his idea of a vacation—a week in the woods. All that activity left its mark on him. I remember the first time I saw him in plain clothes rather than his cassock. It was only then that I realized how strong and well built he actually was. Cassocks can hide an awful lot.

Physical activity was a huge part of John Paul II's life. He wasn't about to give it up as pope. He knew he needed it in order to have the strength and energy to meet the many demands placed upon him. Accordingly, he horrified some at the Vatican when he would jog through the Vatican gardens or sneak out with his closest aide, then Monsignor, now Cardinal Stanislaw Dziwisz, to go skiing. He also raised a few eyebrows when he had a pool built at the papal summer residence. When some questioned the cost of the pool, he famously replied, "It's cheaper than another conclave."

Later, after the pool was built, he noticed that he was the only one using it. He urged the staff and the Swiss Guards to take advantage of it as well. When one of his aides objected that this would disrupt the pope's swimming schedule, John Paul just laughed and said that having lived with university students for so many years, he thought he could fend for himself.

One of the pope's other great loves was music. In order to continue enjoying live performances, he began inviting performers to come to him. He also launched the Vatican Christmas concert series, which brought pop artists from around the world to the

Vatican to raise money for charity. No matter who was performing, John Paul always made a point to greet the artist personally.

The pope worked equally hard to maintain his friendships and relationships. One of his greatest joys as a priest and bishop had always been working closely with his students, and so once he became pope he began a summer school of sorts at Castel Gandolfo. Every year, scholars would be invited to these small conferences, and the pope would personally lead the discussions.

He also went out of his way to receive his friends and former classmates when they were in Rome. He was particularly fond of his schoolmates from Wadowice, the village where he grew up. When it came time for their school reunion, they sent him the invitation, but with little hope that he could come. John Paul, however, surprised them. Not by coming to Poland—he knew that would be too difficult to arrange—but instead by offering to host the reunion in his own dining room at the Vatican.

In all that, John Paul showed me that he knew what so many of us don't: True success can't be had without balance. Like a runner who needs to use both his legs to reach the finish line, we all need to attend to both our work life and personal life if we want to attain our goals. We need to find the balance between work and play, quarterly goals and time spent with friends and family. We need to relax, to cultivate interests and passions outside the office. If we don't, something inside us withers and dies. We may make millions, but without balance, we will still be failures.

All Work and No Play

During my time at the Vatican, I saw how well John Paul II balanced the demands of his papacy with the people and activities he most enjoyed. I saw it, and I admired it. But after I left his service, I did a terrible job of imitating it. For nearly fifteen years, I focused on work to the exclusion of almost everything else. The more responsibility I was given at work, the more I neglected my personal life and interests. Family birthdays came and went. Anniversaries, vacations, even the holidays—I gave them all up for work. Slowly, I began to burn out.

I lost my energy and enthusiasm. I lost the reason for why I was doing what I was doing. I also started to lose friends and lose contact with people for whom I cared deeply. By the time the rug was pulled out from underneath me in 2000, I had forgotten how to have fun. I also had become deeply lonely.

Stealing from Peter to Pay Paul

I, however, was among the lucky ones. I didn't, for example, lose my wife, which happens to be a fairly common fate in the upper echelons of the corporate world. Not long ago, I was at a conference where one of the speakers was a professor from (and graduate of) Harvard Business School. During his talk, he lamented how at every class reunion, more and more of his classmates are divorced. He also explained how every year he challenges his students by presenting three questions they'll need to answer as they enter the business world: (1) How can I be sure I'll be happy in my career? (2) How can I ensure that my relationships become an enduring source of happiness? And (3) How can I stay out of jail?

That professor knows what his students don't. Answering those questions isn't as easy as they think it will be. It requires all that we've talked about thus far—an understanding of vocation, prayer, ethics, the right use of free will, attentiveness to the future and to the moment, knowledge of your team, and the ability to act rightly. But it also requires being able to walk away from the office, away from work and stress and deadlines, and enjoy the rest of what life has to offer. That's difficult. Attaining balance is difficult. Occasionally you run across people who invest too much time in personal matters and can't hold up the work end of the equation. But more often than not, it's the personal side that suffers. Relationships, interests, a prayer life—all that gets sacrificed on the altar of short term profit.

But the truth of the matter is, you can't steal from Peter to pay Paul. The less happy you are at home, the less effective you are at work. Likewise, the less rest you get at night and on weekends, the less efficient you are during the workweek. An inability to find balance in life costs you professionally, as well as personally. It's like that runner we talked about earlier. He can try hopping to the finish line if he wants, but he's not going to win any races that way. The only way to cross the finish line first is to run on both legs. That's what balance is.

So, how do you find it?

Living Balance in Everyday Life

All Things in Moderation

You've heard it before, and it's true: All things in moderation. That's the first key to living a balanced life. When applied to work and your personal life it means pretty much the same thing as when it is applied to diet. Consider eating in moderation: should you eat carrots or cookies? The two aren't mutually exclusive. Over the long-term, most people can't eat only one. You need both carrots and cookies in a balanced diet, and you need both work and a personal life in order to become the person God created you to be. They are intended, in fact, to be complementary, each building on the other and enriching the other.

John Paul understood that. That's why he made time each day for the essentials—prayer, sleep, meals, work, and exercise. He never skipped any of those things. That's also why his week and his month always included scheduled time for recreation—time for reading, listening to music, and staying in touch with friends. It's why annually there were always vacations—extended periods of relaxation where he could do what he loved the most with those whom he cared about the most. John Paul II knew that only by making time for everything in his schedule could he do what was expected of him as pope and do it well.

In the sixth century, Saint Benedict said pretty much the same thing when he was writing out the rule for his monks. "Let all things be done with moderation"[22] he writes. According to Benedict, everything must be given its due, but only its due. There should be something of everything and not too much of anything. Because he was focused on the life of religious men, the balance he was trying to help them find was between work and prayer. That balance was necessary, he believed, because each activity supported and illuminated the other. We need prayer, he said, in order to understand why we're working, just as we need work to help us achieve the order and harmony that sustains our prayer lives. Likewise, he believed that the monks needed to learn to approach prayer with the same determination with which they approached work, recognizing that perfection in anything requires practice.

Benedict also had strong opinions about the rest of what went on in a monk's life. Eating, drinking, sleeping, relaxing, hospitality—all of that was accounted for in his rule. Each of those activities, he asserted, was important to a well-ordered life, as long as they were enjoyed in moderation. To indulge in any at the expense of the others, was asking for trouble.

Benedict's wisdom works just as well for executives in the twenty-first century as it did for monks in the sixth century. In order to be successful, you need to see your work and personal life as two sides of the same coin, as mutually supportive, not mutually exclusive realities. You also need to make sure you schedule time for all that goes into a healthy, happy, productive life. That includes the essential activities for healthy bodies—eating, sleeping, and exercising—as well as the essential activities for healthy souls—spending time with family and friends, praying, reading, and watching the occasional movie or basketball game.

When you approach life with the attitude of "all things in moderation," you avoid the anxiety that comes with feeling like you'll never be able to do something you care about. You also avoid overindulging in something that you don't often get to do. You don't sleep too much on the weekends, because you get plenty of sleep during the week. You don't eat too much at dinner, because you made sure to eat breakfast and lunch. You don't spend every night working late at the office, because you know you'll be back there tomorrow and the budget you're working on isn't going anywhere.

Basically, the "all things in moderation" approach forces you to step back from the urgent concerns of each moment and get a bird's eye view of life. It helps you distinguish between the important and the urgent, to recognize what really needs to be done now and what can wait until later. It's an attitude that stems panic and gives you the courage to face problems, not run from them. It also helps you live in the moment.

Moments of Joy

When you have the weight of other people's futures on your shoulders, it's easy to spend much of your time focused on the future. That's natural, but not always helpful. Many of the CEOs I know, myself included, spend so much time worrying about the future, that we're not always able to enjoy the present. We miss out on what God is offering us right now—small moments of beauty, joy, and peace—because we're worried about problems that haven't yet revealed themselves. We are, in the biblical sense, borrowing trouble from tomorrow.

John Paul II didn't live that way. He didn't spend so much time worrying about tomorrow that he forgot to enjoy the day. He certainly didn't wait until he checked off everything on his "to-do" list to relax and do the things he loved. He did them as he went along, and in that, he found the grace, wisdom, and strength necessary for facing the very real problems that the future did hold.

In that, he was imitating God the Father. God rejoices, Jesus tells us, when one lost sheep, one prodigal son, one precious coin is found. He doesn't wait until all the sheep come home or all problems of the world have been solved. God, in fact, doesn't think about the future at all. That's because to God there is no future.

There is no past. He exists in eternity, outside of time. He lives in the eternal now. He rejoices in the eternal now. He invites us to rejoice along with him in the eternal now.

That doesn't mean that God's just going with the flow and not attending to any plan. If anyone knows how to attend to a plan, it's God. He's the original master planner. But *now* is part of the plan. For us, it's the only part of the plan we can do anything about. We can't change the past. We can't control the future. All we can do is respond to the present challenges and present graces.

In his book, *The Screwtape Letters*, C.S. Lewis does a great job of synthesizing this idea. There, the book's narrator, the demon Screwtape, explains to a lesser demon, Wormwood, the following truth about God and men:

> He therefore, I believe, wants them to attend chiefly to two things, to eternity itself and to the point in time which they call the Present. For the Present is the point at which time touches eternity…Gratitude looks to the Past and love to the Present; fear, avarice, lust, and ambition look ahead…He does not want men to give the future their hearts, to place their treasure in it.[23]

"For the present is the point at which time touches eternity." That line is worth repeating. What Lewis essentially says is that it's in the present moment that God asks you to be with him, to love him, to rejoice with him. All the little moments of beauty and delight that come your way each and every day—newly fallen snow, reading in bed with your children, sitting by the fireside with your spouse, or eating ice cream on a hot summer's day—are invitations from him to do just that. If you miss those invitations, you miss him.

That's another reason why cultivating a daily prayer life is so important. The more you learn to hear God's voice, the more clearly you see those invitations for what they are and the more readily you accept them. The more you accept the momentary graces and joys God offers you, the less susceptible you are to anxiety, insecurity, and all the other fears that can enslave you. The more you relish the joys of the moment, the freer you are.

Giving Thanks

Gratitude and joy go hand in hand. The more grateful you are, the more joy you experience. Likewise, the more grateful you are for what you have, the less likely you are to ignore those gifts or take them for granted. In other words, when you truly appreciate your life, you're not going to spend the whole of it at the office. Like most things, however, gratitude takes practice. Just as you have to train your will to choose and act rightly, you also have to train your soul to be thankful. You have to work at it. That requires a few things.

First, it requires an active prayer life. You have to know that you're grateful to Someone. You have to know Whom to thank. Second, it requires humility. You have to acknowledge your own littleness and helplessness in the grand scheme of things. You have to see that even the things you seem to have accomplished on your own are really the work of God, who gave you your abilities and natural virtues in the first place. Third, you have to recognize that your trials and sorrows are also gifts. God has permitted you to experience them because in his all-loving, all-knowing way, he sees how they will help bring you real and lasting joy.

Once you recognize those things, make a daily habit of thanking God for all the blessings he's bestowed upon you. One way to do this is to begin your prayers each morning with an Act of Thanksgiving. You can also do this after Communion or at the end of the day. I've personally found it helpful to make a list of blessings. It's never anything complicated. Sometimes it's nothing more than a brief list of words in a notebook. Other times, I focus on a certain area of my life—work, home, etc.—or on a specific person—a boss or employee. Just by sitting down with pen and paper and challenging myself to come up with twenty or thirty things for which I'm grateful, I've trained myself to recognize how blessed I am. Once I've taken the time to write out twenty or thirty different gifts God has given me, it's hard to stay negative about anyone or anything.

This also makes it hard to give in to anxiety about the future. The more grateful you become, the more you recognize that you are not the master of your universe. Try as you might, you can't control the future, and no matter how hard you work or how much you sacrifice, you can't control what will eventually come of your work and sacrifices. That knowledge is tremendously freeing. It reminds you to focus on what you can control, and it helps you entrust the future and all your anxieties about it to God. You do what you can, and then head home to throw snowballs with the kids, leaving the rest to God.

If you don't know that an all-loving, all-powerful, ever-merciful God is ultimately the one calling the shots, there's no way you can find balance. There's no way you can walk away from the office and make time to pray and play. You're too busy trying to save the world or the company on your own. But when you know he's there, when you know there's someone far wiser and more capable than you, someone in whom you can place your trust, you can relax. You can find balance. You can make it to the finish line.[24]

***

Of all the lessons I learned from John Paul II, enjoying life and finding balance has been the hardest. It takes a lot of planning and a lot of focus. It also, for me, requires an annual trip to the circus. That too was something I learned from the pope.

In 1982, well before I arrived at the Vatican, the Great Moscow Circus was on a four-month tour of Italy when it received an unexpected invitation: His Holiness, Pope John Paul II, wanted the circus to perform for him in St. Peter's Square.

This request was surprising on many levels. First, only months before, John Paul had nearly been killed by an assassin's bullet. His convalescence was a long one, and papal audiences had been put on hold indefinitely, pending the pope's full recovery.

Second, this was the Great Moscow Circus, the pride of the Soviet Union—the atheist, communist Soviet Union. No Soviet delegation had ever so much as stepped foot into the Vatican. Regardless of whether or not the government granted them permission to perform, the request was unprecedented.

Finally, this was the pope asking, the man tasked with shepherding hundreds of millions of souls. Surely he had more important things to do than watch bears dance in St. Peter's Square?

John Paul II, however, saw things differently. Not only did he know that it was through laughter and shared enjoyment of a thing, not diplomatic negotiations and summits, that relationships were built, but he also knew that he needed laughter and enjoyment. He needed those things in order to be a good pope. Only through finding the right balance of work and relaxation, could he be effective in his work.

So John Paul II invited the circus to the Vatican. When an answer was slow in coming, he sent an emissary to the Soviet Embassy to stress that it was his personal desire for the circus to perform. When Vatican officials protested about the possible dangers of live animals performing in front of the pope, he waived aside all the protocols that would have prevented the performance. The pope also agreed that there would be no talk of politics or war at the audience (this was not long after Soviet troops invaded Afghanistan). This was, he promised the Soviets, an event intended to celebrate life and friendship among peoples, nothing more.

Over fifty thousand people attended the circus in St. Peter's Square that day in March. It was the first audience since the assassination attempt, but not a word was breathed of politics. The pope also spared circus performers the dilemma of how to greet him (the bowing and kissing of the pope's ring was something

Soviet atheists could not do) by greeting each performer with two outstretched hands. He wasn't trying to make any political points that day. He was, like everyone else, a spectator enjoying himself, laughing at Mashka the dancing bear, marveling at the acrobatics, applauding the trained horses.

It was a good day at the Vatican, a great day even, and that wasn't in spite of the fact that pope took the time to laugh and relax. It was because of it.

The New "To-Do" List

1. Determine who the five to ten most important people in your life are. (If you have children, you might expand the number by however many kids you have.) Ask yourself what small thing you can do to bring them joy every day or week. Then, in the next thirty days, do it.

2. Start keeping a personal log of God's small wonders, small messages that he gives you every day. Think of it as a gratitude log. Review it daily and rejoice as you give thanks.

3. Think of the activities you enjoy most. Pick four, then make room in your calendar to do each one sometime during the next thirty days.

4. Diligently use up your vacation time every year. No excuses.

5. Make Sundays truly a day of rest. That means no "for profit" work. Instead go to Church, and then spend the rest of the day with family or friends. Try the concept of finding ways to purposefully "waste time" with them ("Wasting" that is, from a purely productivity-driven point of view). Sit and watch the sunset, play with sand at the beach, just sit and be together, try to create a new game with each other.

Questions for Reflection

1. How good are you at "taking care of yourself," e.g., eating, sleeping, and exercising regularly? Which of the daily essentials is the first to go when things get stressful? In the long run, does that help or hurt your end objectives?

2. What is the last vacation you took? Did you work during the vacation? Check email or answer the cell phone? If no, what were the benefits of that? If yes, how did that affect your vacation? In the end, was it worth it?

3. Look into the future—thirty, forty, fifty years down the road, long past retirement. What do you want your life to look like then? What do you want to be known for? Who do you want to be with? How is the way you're living your life now getting you there? Are the decisions you make with your time moving you closer to or farther away from that goal?

Chapter Nine

Live Detachment:
Intentional Humility and Poverty

"Blessed are the poor in spirit, for theirs is the kingdom of heaven."
Matthew 5:3

In old age, how should one face the inevitable decline of life? How should one act in the face of death? The believer knows that his life is in the hands of God…and he accepts from God the need to die…Man is not the master of life, nor is he the master of death. In life and in death, he has to entrust himself completely to the "good pleasure of the Most High," to his loving plan.
—Blessed John Paul II

W hen I left John Paul II in 1988, he seemed at the height of his strength—fit, active, and full of life. He looked every inch the leader, and his energy was seemingly boundless. But appearances can be deceiving. Even then, complications from the assassin's bullet were slowly stealing his vigor and strength. It was as if the bullet was still ricocheting inside his body, wounding him again and again. None of us knew that. John Paul II bore all his pain quietly, and his sufferings remained, for a time, invisible.

That, however, could only go on for so long. Throughout the 1990s, old age came quickly for the pope who once seemed so young. By 2000, his infirmities were painfully apparent. With each passing day, he grew a little bit weaker. First, it was just the trembling of his hand. Then he had trouble controlling his neck

Epigraph. Encyclical Letter on the Value and Inviolability of Human Life *Evangelium Vitae* (March 25, 1995), 46.

muscles. He slowly became more hunched over, and breathing became more difficult. Eventually the simplest of tasks—speaking and swallowing—required considerable effort.

In some ways, there was nothing remarkable about that. The pope had Parkinson's Disease. He suffered what all who have the disease suffer. He also suffered much of what the very old and the very ill suffer.

But those millions were not the pope. They were not great and powerful leaders of worldwide institutions. Their suffering was not broadcast on a daily basis for all the world to see.

That's not to say that great leaders haven't suffered before. They have. But none have done it so publicly. FDR spent the entirety of his presidency paralyzed from the waist down. He kept that fact from the public, however, refusing to be photographed or filmed in his wheelchair. Similarly, Josef Stalin was a tiny man with a shrunken right hand, but he insisted on being photographed and painted in such a way that he appeared massive and whole. At least four artists who got it wrong were shot.

What set John Paul II apart from those men and others like them was that he never tried to hide his suffering. He wasn't ashamed of it. He didn't think it made him less of a man or less of a leader. He saw meaning in his pain. He believed it had value. He wanted to share that with the world. He wanted to remind us that aging and illness are part of what it means to be human, and that suffering, when accepted, becomes an almost limitless source of grace.

Like the rest of the world, I watched that slow decline on television and in the newspapers. I also heard about it from my friends at the Vatican. By the time he played his closing scene for the world, sitting silently at the window of his study overlooking St. Peter's Square, while the crowds cheered below, everyone who watched, myself included, understood what he was trying to tell us. We understood then, if we didn't before, that a person's dignity doesn't come from what they've accomplished or what they have.

It's not about abilities, gifts, talents, possessions, power, health, or beauty. It's simply about being human. By the mere fact of our existence, we matter.

It took great courage to teach the world that lesson as John Paul II taught it. It also took a spirit of detachment. In order to not just preach about human dignity in the midst of suffering, but to openly embody it, John Paul II had to let go of every shred of human pride. He had to embrace his littleness, his dependence on God. His ability to do that wasn't the work of a moment. It was the work of a lifetime—a lifetime of letting go of pride and letting go of possessions.

Day in and day out, John Paul II practiced humility and intentional poverty. He was able to be the kind of leader God called him to be in those final years, a leader who embodied the very things he worked so hard to accomplish.

Detaching from Pride

St. Augustine once wrote, "Should you ask me, 'What is the first thing in a virtuous life?' I should reply, the first, second, and the third thing therein—nay, all is humility."[25]

The opposite of what Augustine said is also true. At the root of vice is humility's opposite: pride.

Pride, after all, was man's original sin. Adam and Eve wanted to be like gods. They wanted to be their own god. They neither trusted nor obeyed, to our great cost.

We do a good job of imitating Adam and Eve. In my own life, pride has been at the source of so many of the struggles I've faced, including the downfall of several companies. We thought we were the reason for our success. We took all the credit when things went right. We started to believe our own press. We ignored the advice of others, became self-righteous and self-centered. We let our pride blind us to the truth of the situation, to our own weaknesses, and to our dependence in all things on God's grace. So, like Adam and Eve, we fell.

Pride is so insidious because it eats away at the truth of who we are—creatures dependent upon a Creator. This sin goes to the heart of our human identity and therefore can be found in every human endeavor. Pride can destroy marriages, friendships, companies, and careers. Empires have fallen because of pride. We insist that we're right, no matter how wrong we are. We ignore wise counsel, refuse to ask for help, and lie about our weaknesses. Pride is what blinds us to the gifts that other people have and are.

Humility is pride's opposite. It doesn't necessarily mean you think badly of yourself. It means you think rightly of yourself. Or, as "One Minute Manager" Kenneth Blanchard once wrote, "People with humility don't think less of themselves. They think of themselves less."[26]

To reject pride and embrace humility is to understand who you are and who made you. It is to cultivate both dependence on God and a spirit of obedience to his will. It's also to see your desires as secondary and the needs of others as primary.

To John Paul II, the virtue of humility seemed to come as naturally as breathing. Maybe that wasn't always the case. There must have been times where he had to do great battle with his will. As a young man serving under him, I never saw that. He was always more interested in others than he was in himself. Hence our conversation on that lonely Christmas Eve in 1986, where he noticed my tears.

Humility is also what gave John Paul II the courage to live his illness in front of the television cameras. He was weak. He was suffering. What was the point of hiding that? God knew it. God permitted it. Hiding what God permitted, what God willed, would have been an act of disobedience, done in the spirit of pride, to make himself seem stronger, better, than he actually was.

Importantly, humility is what led John Paul II to do things such as forgive his would-be assassin, Ali Agca, and greet Poland's communist dictator, General Wojciech Jaruzelski, with as much kindness as he greeted its first democratically elected president, Lech Walesa.

The pope didn't have to visit Agca in prison, let alone advocate publicly for the man's eventual release. He also didn't have to treat Jaruzelski, the man responsible for so much poverty, suffering, and death in his beloved homeland, with respect. John Paul II could have said one word and Agca would never have seen the light of day again. He could have lifted one finger, and all of Poland would have launched into armed rebellion. He did neither. The reason for that was his humility. John Paul didn't nurse anger. He didn't hold on to resentment. He didn't let his pride rule his better judgment, judgment that told him forgiveness, respect, and peace would ultimately bear more fruit that any acts of vengeance or rebellion.

Because John Paul II didn't consider himself to be great, he became great. He made decisions based on wise counsel. He had a proper view of his own strengths and weaknesses. He always had the help he needed, both from others and from God.

Learning to Let Things Go
To become a great leader in your businesses or market, you need to learn to let things go. Your decisions have a profound impact on others, and you have to make sure that your ego isn't calling the shots. You can't simply follow your own whims and desires, and you can't be afraid to face your weaknesses, let them be known, and ask for help. No man is Superman. Not even John Paul II. We all need help. We all need grace. We all need to be willing to go to men and God to get it.

We also need to be willing to give people second chances. People make mistakes. Big mistakes. I found that firing someone out of anger because they messed up is usually a mistake. It's a decision based on pride, and such decisions usually backfire. After all, the person with whom you replace the employee could make the same mistake. There's no guarantee that the replacement will never make errors. On the other hand, chances are good that the person whose mistake you forgive will learn from what happened and never make that mistake again. They'll also likely remain fiercely loyal to you and the company.

This doesn't mean that you never dismiss employees. If someone honestly can't do their job, dismissing them is actually the most loving thing you can do. You're freeing them to go and do what God made them to do. It also doesn't mean you can't put people on performance plans or ask them to meet difficult goals. Being a humble leader is not about holding hands with your employees and singing "Kumbaya." It does require that you have the courage to forgive and that you treat your employees as equals. It does require you to admit when you're wrong and get the best help you can.

I know that letting go of pride and embracing humility can be terrifying at first. It involves making oneself vulnerable and letting go of the control we think we have. In the corporate world, where most people have constructed thick shells of emotional and professional armor to hide all signs of weakness, practicing humility can feel decidedly counterintuitive. But it is the only way to become a truly great leader.

If you have any doubts, consider this: Who, besides maybe Kim Jong-Il, thinks Josef Stalin was a greater man than John Paul II?

Which man was afraid to show his weaknesses and which man put them on display for all the world to see?

Detaching From Possessions

Humility and poverty go hand in hand. Not because being poor makes you humble, but rather because being intentionally detached from commercial success or failure brings the same freedom and serenity that having an accurate understanding of your place in the universe brings. John Paul II was a prime example of this.

Karol Wojtyla did not belong to a religious order such as the Augustinians, Dominicans, or Franciscans. He was a diocesan priest, which means he never formally took a vow of poverty. He lived poverty nonetheless. He never had a bank account or a credit card. He never even owned anything for very long. His friends used to lament that as soon as they gave him a gift, he would give it away. He did that as a priest and as a bishop, and he still did that when he became pope.

At the end of every day in the Vatican, one of the Swiss Guards would go to the papal apartments to deliver the list of attendees for the next morning's Mass. The guard would usually go straight to the kitchen, where the sisters who attended the pope were, and often the pope would be there sitting and talking with them. If the pope was there, the guard never left empty handed. The pope would say something like, "Didn't someone just give us a case of wine?" The sisters would reply yes, and tell the pope where it was. Then the pope would tell the guard, "Go get that and give it to the guards downstairs. Give them my greetings."

Many of the gifts the pope didn't manage to give away during the course of the year were saved and distributed to the Swiss Guards and all other Vatican employees at Christmas. He kept almost nothing for himself. Even living in the midst of a palace as sumptuous as the Vatican, he found a way to live poverty. For example, his personal apartments went untouched during all the years he lived there. No improvements or renovations were ever made. He didn't want them, and he didn't need them.

The point of this poverty, however, wasn't to possess nothing. It was, in part, to practice a detachment from the cares of the world, cares that can get in the way of seeing and valuing spiritual realities. In this life, it's easy to become focused on the visible trappings of success or feel as if money and things are the goals of work. If you do that, however, you run the risk of letting your desire for things get in the way of your desire for God. You can make compromises, big compromises, in order to attain them. You can make the pursuit of them your greatest good. Cultivating a detachment from those things—not buying what you don't need, giving readily and quickly to those who do—acts as a check on that tendency. It frees you to make the right decisions and follow God's will, regardless of the cost.

It also builds trust in God.

Jesus chided those who fretted too much about clothes and things, noting that if God could provide so well for the lilies of the field, he could provide for men too. He wanted his disciples to trust that God, their loving Father, would provide for all they truly needed. He wants the same for you. Intentional poverty is an act of humility. It's recognizing that there is someone else in charge who is looking out for you, and that your welfare depends far more upon his grace, than on your ability to store up riches.

How, then, shall you live? This does not mean that you must work for free; it doesn't mean you should not pursue a promotion or salary increase. You are made for excellence and pursuing these goals through virtue can be one way to pursue excellence at work. The question that addresses intentional poverty is rather how you regard the money you make and what you use it for. Do you believe that you are better than someone who earns less? Do you spend your money on self-indulgences? Do you drive the latest new car every three years? Do you belong to the top-of-the-line golf club? Do you give freely to worthy causes? Do you see money as a means to an end or as the end goal? It is okay to have nice possessions and to enjoy the fruits of one's labor. The key question about intentional poverty is not about how much you have; it's about how your soul sees it. It is worth contemplating this answer for some time, and letting your behavior speak rather than your arguments. I spent many years lying to myself about the true role money played in my life.

John Paul practiced intentional poverty because he already knew his answers to those questions. He already didn't care all that much, one way or the other, about material possessions. The gifts he gave weren't that important to him—not the receiving of them and not the giving of them. The poverty he lived was spiritual, even more than it was material. He was so focused on God and the transcendent, so aware of his own littleness and dependency on grace, that he simply didn't give things that much thought. The only gift he really cared about was the gift of self. That was the most precious gift he gave others and that was the most precious gift he knew he could receive from others.

John Paul II understood what truly mattered in this life. That doesn't mean he didn't have favorite foods or appreciate beauty when he saw it. He saw the usefulness of things and was grateful for all that he did have. But those things had no power over him. In and of themselves, they didn't interest him. They didn't control him. He was free—free to serve, free to love, free to lead.

Pursuing True Poverty

All leaders need to seek that same freedom. That doesn't mean you can't invest for your retirement or buy your kids Christmas presents. It doesn't mean you need to give away every gift that comes your way. As a parent or provider, you can't do those things and still meet your responsibilities. Intentional poverty looks different for a husband and father of five living in the world than it does for a celibate pope living in the Vatican or women religious in a cloistered convent.

At least, it looks different from the outside. From the inside, it's pretty much the same. You may have to own a car, but you don't have to confuse your identity or worth with the type of car you drive. You may have to save up for retirement, but you don't have to center your life on building up a retirement savings account. The sun shouldn't rise and set according to your investment portfolio. Your world shouldn't end if your business does.

The goal is to make the acquisition of spiritual wealth, not material wealth, the focus of your life. As part of that, when you face a choice between making a profit and being honest, you have to go with the being honest option. The moral action always has to come first. And it will, if that's what matters more.

To develop detachment from material possessions, it helps to give generously. As we discussed earlier, the act of doing something

135

can help produce the corresponding virtue. The more you give, the more generous you become, and the less attached you grow to what you posses. Similarly, the more you give away what's yours, the more you realize that none of it was yours in the first place. It came to you through God's grace, and through God's grace you give it to another.

It also helps to consciously go without, forgoing upgrades to new cars, televisions, and the latest gadgets that you don't need, passing up second helpings or dessert at meals, wearing last year's suit instead of shelling out hundreds or thousands for a new one. All of those are little acts of self-deprivation, but together they help break the bonds that attach you to material wealth.

At the same time, you need to pursue spiritual wisdom: reading the Bible, attending Church, and receiving the Sacraments. You need to study the lives of the saints and the teachings of the Church. You need to grow in your knowledge of your faith, so that you can grow in your understanding of it. The more you know, the more you understand. The more you understand, the more you believe. The more you believe, the more clearly you see what matters in life.

Intentional poverty, like humility, isn't easy to pursue. The line between valuing possessions rightly and too much or too little is a fine one. When you find a way to stay on the right side of the line, you find the same freedom John Paul II had—again, the freedom to love, the freedom to serve, and the freedom to lead.

***

Over the years, I've heard a lot of great stories about John Paul II from friends at the Vatican and others who knew him personally. One of my favorites is this one from Scott Hahn.[27] I repeat it here, because I can think of no greater testimony to the detachment we're all called to possess.

During the later years of John Paul II's papacy, an American priest attended a conference in Rome. On the last day of the conference, he went to a church at midday to pray. As he walked in, he saw the ever-present beggars in front. He stopped, thought he recognized one of them, but dismissed the thought and walked inside. Still, he couldn't help thinking about that beggar, so on his way out, he approached the man.

"Excuse me," he said. "Do I know you?"

The man looked away, but answered, "Yes, we went to seminary together and were ordained together in Rome."

The beggar priest then told the American about how horrific life choices and bad mistakes had poisoned and destroyed his vocation. The priest was devastated, but didn't know what to say and hurried back to the Vatican.

That afternoon, there was an audience with the pope for all the attendees of the conference. The priest could not resist the temptation. As he approached John Paul, he said, "Holy Father, you have to pray for this priest I just saw." And he told him the story.

After the audience, the American went back to that parish looking for the homeless priest. When he found him, he said, "The pope is praying for you."

The beggar just stared at him with a look that said, "Well that's great...whatever good that'll do."

But the priest continued. "That's not all. The pope and his secretary, Bishop Dziwisz, invited the two of us for dinner tonight."

The man protested. He was dirty. He had no decent clothes. But the priest persuaded him with an offer of a shower and the loan of one of his own suits. So they went.

The Swiss Guard on duty let them in, and they were ushered up to the apartment where Bishop Dziwisz greeted them. He then led them into the dining room where the pope was already at table. Everyone exchanged greetings and the first course was served. Then the second course. At the end of the main course, the pope began moving his hand in a motion to Bishop Dziwisz. The American priest didn't understand what the gesture meant, but the bishop did. He got up and said to him: "Please come with me for a moment."

The two left and waited outside. One minute passed, then two, then five, then ten. Finally the bishop seemed to know it was time to go back in. They sat down just in time for dessert.

At the end of the evening, farewells and blessings were exchanged and the two priests walked back down the marble stairs to St. Peter's Square. The American priest, however, was dying of curiosity, so as soon as they came out into the open he turned and asked: "What went on in there?"

The beggar said, "You wouldn't believe it, even if I told you."

"You have to tell me. Try me!" was the American's response.

"Well, as soon as you left the room, John Paul turned to me and said 'Father, would you please hear my confession?' I said, 'Holy Father, I'm not a priest, I'm a beggar.' And the pope responded 'So am I, I am just a beggar. You are a priest. Once a priest, always a priest.'

"'But Holy Father,' I told him, 'I'm not in right standing with the Church!'

"'As the bishop of Rome, I can reinstate you here and now,' was his reply. 'All you have to do is give me consent.'

"How could I withhold consent from the bishop of Rome?" the beggar concluded.

After hearing the story, the American priest said "But we were out there for more than ten minutes. It couldn't have taken that long for him to confess his sins?"

"No," the beggar agreed. "It was over in a couple of minutes. That's when I dropped to my knees and begged him to hear my confession. And he did. Right before you came back in, he asked me where you found me, and upon my telling him, he asked me to report to the pastor there tomorrow. I'll be assigned to that church, and my mission will be reaching out to all of our fellow beggars in that neighborhood. Because that's what all of us are."

St. Benedict's 12 Steps to Humility

Fourteen hundred years ago, St. Benedict developed a 12-step program to help his monks perfect the virtue of humility. It was probably the world's first 12-step program.

In the book, *The Benedictine Rule of Leadership*, Craig and Oliver Galbraith took that 12-step program and adapted it into something practical and useful for leaders today.[28] Here is a summation of what they had to say:

Step 1: Revere the simple rules. Don't speed. Stop at red lights. Meet deadlines.

Step 2: Reject your personal desires. Fast when a little hungry. Avoid impulse buying. Skip dessert.

Step 3: Obey those in positions of authority. Pay your taxes. Follow your confessor's advice. Rewrite the report for your manager. Take the trash out for your wife.

Step 4: Endure affliction. When someone insults you, turn the other cheek. When you're sick, don't whine. When you're snubbed, smile.

Step 5: Confess your weakness. When you're wrong, admit it. When a task at work proves difficult, talk with your manager about what you might be doing wrong. Do an examination of conscience every night. Go to confession.

Step 6: Practice contentment. Drive the old car. Keep the old house. Don't upgrade to the next version of a gadget when the one you have is all you really need.

Step 7: Learn self-reproach: When something goes wrong—at home, at work, with friends—make the first question you ask yourself, "What could I have done differently to prevent this." Be honest with yourself.

Step 8: Obey the common rule. Abide by organization policy faithfully and according to the spirit of the law, not just the letter of the law.

Step 9: Understand that silence is golden. Listen more than you speak. Make your orders few and reasonable.

Step 10: Meditate on humility. Read the Gospels. Study the lives of the saints. Think about the great men and women you've known. How were they humble? What example did they set? How can you imitate them?

Step 11: Speak simply. Talk in a low, quiet voice. Speak gently. Have a kind word for everyone.

Step 12: Be humble in appearance. Dress simply. Eat simply. Cultivate simple hobbies and simple tastes.

Questions for Reflection

1. Describe a situation where your pride has led you to act rashly or wrongly. What were you afraid of? What were the consequences of your actions? To you? To others? How would things have turned out differently if you had taken your own ego out of the equation?

2. To what are you attached? What can't you do without? What things do you find yourself working for or pursuing that aren't really necessary? Why? How might that get you into trouble in the long run?

3. What are three things you can do this month to help you let go of your attachment to your pride and possessions? What are three things you can do every day to do the same?

Conclusion
Back in the Barracks

"Be still, and know that I am God"
"Be still and confess that I am God!"
Psalms 46:10–11 NIV

The call came via email: "Message from the Commander: Ex-Guards Needed For Active Duty."

I was on retreat, and probably shouldn't have been checking my messages to begin with. "I'll only read those that have to do with an emergency," is what I promised myself. But as soon as I saw that tagline, there was no way I wasn't reading further.

The message was a direct request from the Commander of the Swiss Guards. He needed some former guards to come back to the Vatican, just for a few days, and help out the corps during a very busy time. They had thirty-three new recruits to be sworn in and he wanted to find some "ex-guards" to cover for them so they could take some time off after their swearing in to be with their parents and relatives who came to Rome for the occasion. This was the first time in the history of the Guards that they'd made such a request.

I don't think I even finished reading the entire email before I sent my reply: "Tell me when, and I'll be there."

That was in early April. Four weeks later, on May 1, 2009, I arrived back at the barracks of the Swiss Guards in Vatican City. It was twenty years and five months to the day since I left.

In Conversation With Myself

So much had changed for me over the past two decades, but as soon as I stepped foot in those barracks, I felt like I was twenty-two again. There were new guards and a new pope, but other than that, everything felt the same. The barracks, after all, hadn't changed. The atmosphere hadn't changed. The young men, the uniforms they wore, the rooms they lived in, the tasks they performed— all was as it had been. I felt as if I'd traveled to this place via time machine.

As soon as I checked in, I was assigned a room in the barracks, given my bedding, and left to settle in before dinner. There were about thirty of us who responded to the call, many whom I'd known in the old days, so that first dinner felt more like a reunion than anything else. We sat and talked for hours, going over old times, new times, and everything in between. Then we all retired to our quarters. We had a long day coming up, and, actually, none of us were twenty-two anymore.

That night, as I lay in bed, I noticed how the light from St. Peter's Square hit the ceiling of my room. Suddenly waves of memory came crashing over me. It was like I had been transported back in time to my last night at the Vatican twenty years before. I remembered lying awake under this same ceiling watching this same light. I also remembered the fear and anxiety that gripped me then.

I prayed long and hard that night twenty years ago. "Lord, what will you have me do? What will become of me? What are your plans for me." I felt then like I was about to jump off a cliff. I didn't know where I would end up, what I would do, and whom I would do it with. I was leaving to be with Michelle, but I had no idea if that would work out. I didn't know if my time in the Guards would help me in any concrete way once I was back in the real world. I was young, insecure, and unsure of so many things.

As my forty-two-year-old self lay in bed, I could hear once more the prayers of the twenty-two-year-old young man I once had been. I could feel his fear, his excitement, his hope. But I knew what he didn't. I knew the answers. I knew I would marry Michelle, that I would never stop loving her, and that after many long years of waiting God would bless us with a beautiful son to love and raise together. I also knew about the wild roller coaster ride my professional life would be, that there would be incredible highs and terrible lows, but that the whole thing, from start to finish, would bring me closer to God. I also knew how profoundly my time in the Guards and my relationship with John Paul II would shape that ride.

If I could, I would have told him all that. I also would have told him all that I've written in this book: Know how you're called to give your life as a gift. Pray constantly and in all things. Seek to know what's right. Work to choose what's right. Look to the future but live with God in the present. Know and love those who are with you on the journey. Lead by example. Never neglect the most important things in life. Don't invest yourself in that which isn't important.

I would have told him one more thing. I would have told him the key that holds all those other ideas together and directs them to their proper end: Know that what you ultimately want is not physical, not material. If you strip everything else away, you will realize that what your heart really desires is God. It won't rest until it rests in God.

"So do not worry and say, 'What are we to eat?' or 'What are we to drink?' or 'What are we to wear?' All these things the pagans seek. Your heavenly Father knows that you need them all. But seek first the kingdom (of God) and his righteousness, and all these things will be given you besides. Do not worry about tomorrow; tomorrow will take care of itself. Sufficient for a day is its own evil."

Matthew 6:31–34

The Ultimate Objective

Back when I was twenty-two I wanted a lot—money, success, happiness—and I wanted these in about equal measure. My pursuit of these three ends led me in different directions, not all of them good. Eventually I learned that all these things don't actually fulfill you. Each gives you something, but nothing profound and lasting. If I live for eighty or ninety years any one of the worldly achievements only last for a fleeting moment in comparison to my whole life. I found that ultimately there is only one thing worth wanting—to go to heaven and live forever in God's love.

This is too often seen as a cliché, but give this some serious thought. St. Thomas Aquinas described heaven this way: True and perfect light, total fulfillment, everlasting joy, gladness without end, and perfect happiness.[29]

That is the sum total, the perfection of every desire I've ever had. Heaven is where I get to realize in full the beauty and joys of which this earthly life is just a taste. If there is a heaven, and I believe there is, then that's where I want to go and where I want my family, my friends, my co-workers and everyone else to go as well.

This is what John Paul II made me understand: All areas of my life today can be a foretaste of heaven, and they are a training ground to help us get to heaven. Some of the nine principles in this book might inspire you to lead your team in such a way that your work is a help and not a hindrance on that journey. They might help you to make your work sanctifying, both for you and for others.

It takes immense commitment and selfless sacrifice to be the kind of leader John Paul II was. But it also brings a great amount of fulfillment and happiness to your life. You have to be willing to be countercultural, to defy the selfishness paradigm at work. A servant leader like John Paul finds himself by giving of himself and is willing to pay for that sacrifice. On the other hand, you will experience profound accomplishment and satisfaction in doing what you ought to do and not just what you feel like doing. The happiness that comes from helping your employees achieve their personal best, from rewarding your investors with solid long-term financial returns, from doing work that is truly good is immeasurable. It is the kind of happiness that foreshadows heaven. This experience will in turn make you even more committed and excited to pursue your ultimate goal of one day entering into the presence of God forever.

You will of course still be tempted to compromise, to not make the tough calls, to take the easy way out. It will always remain a matter of faith: You've got to want heaven and believe it's attainable in order to follow in the footsteps of the pope and other great Christian leaders. But if you do, oh the difference it makes.

The Temporal Payoff
That difference, however, is not just to you. Companies led by a strong, moral leader perform better in the long run.

This has been demonstrated in recent years by investors such as Joe Ritchie and Tom Monaghan, who've made fortunes by basing their investment decisions on a company CEO's character or values. It's also been demonstrated by the Ethisphere Institute, which regularly ranks the world's most ethical companies. According to *Forbes*, the stock of the top companies ranked by Ethisphere have grown at more than double the rate of the Standard & Poor's 500 over the past five years.[30]

In his book *Spiritual Capital*, Theodore Roosevelt Malloch writes about the impact of "spiritual capital" on companies, describing over fifty companies whose founder or CEO provides spiritually inspired leadership. In the appendix to the book he looks at the financial performance of companies such as Herman Miller, Service Master, Franklin Resources, and others, noting that, "These virtuous companies did well as they did good, outperforming their competitors in many cases on the S&P index, in most cases over the long run."

He concludes by suggesting, "So maybe virtue pays off in more than one way?"[31]

That doesn't mean that virtuous leadership is any guarantee of temporal success. As Michael Novak writes in *Business as a Calling*, virtue doesn't always pay off financially and certainly not in the short term. In fact, it often has costs. For moral reasons alone, however, those costs are well worth paying. As Novak himself said, "A religious and moral business leader has plenty of room to do the right thing and insist on it throughout the company. People employed by the company enjoy knowing that they work for a serious, moral association."[32]

CEOs enjoy running such corporations as well. There's no joy in running a corrupt corporation. There's no joy in compartmentalizing your professional and personal life. There's no joy in thinking such compartmentalization is necessary.

I've known executives who see their work life as an unpleasant distraction from their personal life or who've bought into the idea that virtue and corporate management are intrinsic opposites, that one can't pursue profit and goodness simultaneously. I've also known plenty of executives who see their personal life as an unpleasant distraction from their work life and don't believe in truth, virtue, or goodness at all.

Those ways of thinking are wrong. They're rooted either in a dangerous dualism that separates the spiritual from the material or in a relativism that denies objective reality itself. Both deny truth, and both deny the God who became flesh. They deny the God who worked as a carpenter, sought to earn a profit in his business, and provided for his mother from those earnings. They deny all that the Incarnation made possible for each one of us.

John Paul II didn't deny any of those things. He saw more than just value in work. He saw work as a path to heaven. He saw man becoming more fully and truly man through work. He taught me to see those things as well. It took me longer than I would have liked to learn that lesson. There were plenty of hardships and heartaches until I did. But in the end, it's all been worth it. God outdid my wildest expectations and calmed my deepest fears. He did that, in large part, through the witness of one man. More than anyone else I've ever met, John Paul II showed me what real leadership looks like. He modeled it for me just as he modeled it for the world. That has made all the difference in my life.

Lying in bed that night at the Vatican, I finally understood all that. I completed the prayer of my twenty-two-year-old self with a prayer of praise and thanksgiving. I praised God for giving me the eyes to see what he had for me, and I thanked him for giving me a leader like John Paul II to follow and serve. Then I finally rested, secure in the knowledge of what I wanted and trusting completely in the path that was taking me there, the path shown to me and to you by John Paul II.

Acknowledgments

Conceiving and writing this book has been a long process; the list of those who have contributed would require an entire sequel. Thank you to everyone who has helped in shaping this book, reading the manuscript, making comments, and helping publish and promote it. I never knew that writing a book is a team sport!

Without the unconditional love, support, advice, and enthusiasm of my wife, Michelle, this book could never have been written and published. I love you—always have and always will.

I want to thank my parents for giving me life and being role models of living the Faith.

In gratitude I think of my business partner and friend Mike Fairbanks. Our many conversations helped inspire this book and he welcomed and encouraged the idea of it from the first moment he saw an outline. His creative and critical comments made this book more logical and much more readable.

My sincere thanks go to George Weigel for contributing the introduction and for his guidance and advice throughout this process.

To Bob Allard and Scot Landry, two loyal friends, reliable critics and vigorous supporters. It is a privilege to be your friend!

Profound thanks to Elizabeth Hooper, who read and commented on every page (including many pages now discarded), and whose ideas, suggestions, and warnings have resulted in countless improvements. Her extraordinary persistence and hard work have made this book better than I could have ever made it.

A number of friends and colleagues contributed their advice and assistance. These include Cardinal Peter Turkson and Michael Novak, who gave me greatly valued encouragement and inspiration throughout the process. Thanks also to Peter Gori, O.S.A., Arthur Johnson O.S.A, Rosario and Gerard Schultz, Carmen Lee Schultz, Fr. Roger Landry, Fr. John Grimes, Sebastian Seromik, Magdalena Krzystolik, Thomas Howard, Irene Lagan, Charles Harper, John Lariviere, Kay McAvoy, Jo Tango, Karl and Elizabeth Wirth, Jan-Hein Cremers, Al Lagan, Tim VanDamm, Michael and Catherine Pakaluk, Michael and Caitlin Raeger, Michael Czerny S. J., Patrick Novecosky, Joan Lewis, Tom Peterson, David George, Joe Gemmell, Richard Omohundro, Andy LaVallee, Anna Halpine, Fr. Robert Sirico, Sam Gregg, Michael Miller, Kishore Jayabalan, Cardinal Sean O'Malley, Archbishop James Harvey, Monsignor Camille Perl, The Brotherhood of Hope, Marie Oats, Claire Huang, Mark Wildermuth, Rich Swanson, Martin Doman, Mauro De Lorenzo, Christoph Wassermann, Sr. Catherine O'Connor, David Howlett, David and Angela Franks, Bob Keith, and Mary Matalin.

A big thank you to the Pontifical Swiss Guards for the opportunities, memories, and guidance. Specifically to Commander Daniel Anrig, Vice Commander Christoph Graf, to Matthias Widmer, Michael Widmer, Roland Huwiler, Franziskus Karlen, Bernard Moret, Daniel Wicki, Hermann Baettig, Stefan Meier, Stefan Huesler, Martin Utz, Erwin Niederberger, Frowin Bachmann, Mario Enzler, Roman Fringeli, Andreas Clemenz, Pirmin Zinsli, Graziano Rossi, Giovanni Roggen, and all current and retired Guards. This is not only my story. It's our story. Fifty percent of the royalties due to me personally will be used to support the Swiss Guard's educational needs. *Acriter et Fideliter!*

I wish to thank the entire team at Emmaus Road Publishing for their early show of confidence and their commitment to making this book a reality, especially Michael Sullivan, Emily Stimpson, Shannon Hughes, and Eric Stoutz.

Special thanks and gratitude to Karin Rabensteiner, my niece, for the cover design and for teaching me that design is as important as words.

Profound thanks to the John Templeton Foundation: without their support, many of the ideas in this book could not have percolated.

Thanks to the team at Fresh Tilled Soil for their expertise and patience in working on the book's website thepopeandtheceo.com.

Above all thank you to those who have prayed with me and for me and encouraged me over the years.

Ad Majorem Dei Gloriam

Endnotes

1   Pope John Paul II, Greeting for the Jubilee of Workers (May 1, 2000), no. 3, available from http://www.vatican.va.

2   Pope John Paul II, Homily for the Jubilee of the Apostolate of the Laity (November 26, 2000), no. 3, available from http://www.vatican.va.

3   Karol Wojtyla, *Love And Responsibility* (San Francisco: Ignatius Press, 1981), 82.

4   Wojtyla, *Love And Responsibility*, 82.

5   Wojtyla, *Love And Responsibility*, 257.

6   Karol Wojtyla, *The Way To Christ: Spiritual Exercises* (San Francisco: HarperOne, 1994), 19-20.

7   See, for example, Wojtyla, *The Way To Christ: Spiritual Exercises*, 6.

8   In 1979, two years before his attempted assassination of Pope John Paul II, Ali Agca assassinated Abdi Pekçi, a Turkish journalist and human rights activist. In 2000, after a pardon for the assassination attempt, Agca was extradited to Turkey were he was imprisoned for the murder of Pekçi and for other crimes.

9   Wojtyla, *The Way To Christ: Spiritual Exercises*, 67.

10 For an in-depth treatment of John Paul II's and Ronald Reagan's opposition to communism, see John O'Sullivan's *The President, the Pope, and the Prime Minister: Three Who Changed the World* (Washington, DC: Regnery Publishing, 2006) and George Weigel's *The End and the Beginning: Pope John Paul II, The Victory of Freedom, The Later Years, The Legacy* (New York: Doubleday, 2010).

11 Wojtyla, *Love and Responsibility*, 41.

12 That framework is also called the "Personalistic Norm." "The person is a good towards which the only proper and adequate attitude is love." Negatively defined, the Personalistic Norm "states that the person is the kind of good which does not admit of use and cannot be treated as an object of use and as such the means to an end" (Wojytla, *Love and Responsibility*, 41).

13 Pope John Paul II, Encyclical Letter on the Redemption and the Dignity of Man *Redemptoris Hominis* (March 4, 1979), no. 15, available from http://www.vatican.va/holy_father/john_paul_ii/encyclicals/documents/hf_jp-ii_enc_04031979_redemptor-hominis_en.html.

14 John Paul II, Address to the Diplomatic Corps (January 13, 2003), 2, available from http://www.vatican.va/holy_father/john_paul_ii/speeches/2003/january/documents/hf_jp-ii_spe_20030113_diplomatic-corps_en.html.

15 cf. Psalm 1:1–6: "Happy those who do not follow the counsel of the wicked, Nor go the way of sinners, nor sit in company with scoffers. Rather, the law of the LORD is their joy; God's law they study day and night. They are like a tree planted near streams of water, that yields its fruit in season; Its leaves never wither; whatever they do prospers. But not the wicked! They are like chaff driven by the wind. Therefore the wicked will not survive judgment, nor will sinners in the assembly of the just. The LORD watches over the way of the just, but the way of the wicked leads to ruin."

16 John Paul II's last will is available from http://www.vatican.va/gpII/documents/testamento-jp-ii_20050407_en.html.

17 As I heard Professor Kenneth Goodpaster of the University of St. Thomas say.

18 Eric Krell, "Do They Trust You?," *HRMagazine*, June 1, 2006, http://www.allbusiness.com/sector-92-public-administration/administration-human/1180922-1.html.

19 John Paul II, *Crossing The Threshold of Hope* (New York: Alfred A. Knopf, Inc., 1994), available from http://frcoulter.com/books/CrossingThresholdHope/chap19.html.

20 Aristotle, Rhetoric 1380b36–1381a2.

21 Wojtyla, *Love And Responsibility*, 83.

22 Henry Bettenson, ed., *Documents of the Christian Church* (New York: Oxford University Press, 1970), 116-128; XLVIII.

23 C.S. Lewis, *The Screwtape Letters* (New York: McMillan Publishing, 1982), 67-69.

24 cf. 1 Corinthians 9:24–27: "Do you not know that the runners in the stadium all run in the race, but only one wins the prize? Run so as to win. Every athlete exercises discipline in every way. They do it to win a perishable crown, but we an imperishable one. Thus I do not run aimlessly; I do not fight as if I were shadowboxing. No, I drive my body and train it, for fear that, after having preached to others, I myself should be disqualified."

25 Craig S. Galbraith and Oliver Galbraith, *The Benedictine Rule of Leadership: Classic Management Secrets You Can Use Today* (Avon, MA: Adams Media 2004), 115.

26 Kenneth Blanchard, *The Power of Ethical Management* (New York: William Morrow & Co., 1988), 49.

27 Scott Hahn, "On the Lord's Prayer" (address to the Boston Catholic Men's conference, March 4, 2006).

28 Galbraith and Galbraith, *The Benedictine Rule of Leadership*, 119–122.

29 "Thanksgiving after Mass," available from http://www.ibreviary.com/m/preghiere.php?id=207.

30 Sharon Allen, "The New ROE: Return On Ethics," *Forbes* (July 21. 2009), available from www.forbes.com/2009/07/21/business-culture-corporate-citizenship-leadership-ethics.html.

31 Theodore Roosevelt Malloch, *Spiritual Enterprise* (New York: Encounter Books, 2008), 147.

32 Michael Novak, *Business As A Calling: Work and The Examined Life* (New York: The Free Press, 1986), 168. Novak has a set of very useful lists of internal and external corporate responsibilities in that same book on page 134 and on, which I recommend to interested readers.